First published 1944
Reprinted 1970 by permission of
Cambridge University Press

ISBN: 0-208-00993-0
Library of Congress Catalog Card Number: 76-121754
Printed in the United States of America

THE ENGLISHMAN
& HIS HISTORY

THE ENGLISHMAN
AND HIS HISTORY

By

H. BUTTERFIELD

*With a new Preface
by
the Author*

ARCHON BOOKS
1970

TO

MY FATHER

PREFACE — 1970

In 1938, after taking advice, I accepted an invitation to lecture at the universities of Cologne, Bonn, Münster and Berlin. My German correspondent told me that students in his country knew my *Whig Interpretation of History*; and he asked me if I would meet the desire for knowledge about the origin and history of that interpretation. The question was one which I had never considered; and my attempt to meet the request was my first serious engagement with the history of historiography —a branch of scholarship which (in spite of famous interventions by Lord Acton and G.P. Gooch) had then aroused little interest in England and was often regarded as very much a German affair.

It became evident, as I studied the problem which had been presented to me, that the topic concerned the real beginning of "historical interpretation" in England. It further transpired that the story could not be studied as merely the history of a branch of historical scholarship; for in this particular case—or at this particular stage in the development—historical writing was closely connected not only with the living world of contemporary politics but also with the way in which men in general "experienced" the past, the way they felt about it or found themselves committed to it. The whig interpretation which in my view had long been a barrier to historical understanding turned out to have been at one time the initial stage in a general advance. And, what-

ever its place in the history of scholarship, it had been
an important factor in the development not merely of
the whigs but of the whole political tradition—indeed
the political consciousness—of Englishmen. The first
half of the present book is an expanded version of my
German lecture on this subject.

A further impulse from abroad at the same time
awakened my interest in the origin of another aspect of
the whig tradition—one which in the course of time
came again to be regarded not merely as whig but as
national, as British. The hint came from Rapin de Thoy-
ras, whose history of England, when translated from the
French, became a best seller in eighteenth-century England and commanded the field even there until the ad-
vent of David Hume. In 1717 Rapin set out to explain
to Frenchmen the workings of party-politics in England,
and he showed how the leaders of the whigs (unlike their
tory counterparts) had moved away from the fanaticism
of the seventeenth century, pursuing now a careful
policy of moderation and compromise. It seemed to me
that here was an important stage in the transition from
what I should call the politics of the *coup d'état* to the
politics of a stable *régime*—an important aspect of the
history of England in the early decades of the eighteenth
century. The country had had its civil wars and, not
very long ago, had beheaded a king. At the time of the
Exclusion Bill controversy—in the period 1679-81—the
bitterness of political conflict had led some people to
fear a further resort to violence. The mere possibility of
such a disaster had provoked serious reflection about
the events of the previous generation—about the char-

acter of revolutionary politics and the unintended, unpredictable results of the appeal to force. Out of this
reflection on an historical experience new political maxims were being produced. Here, therefore, was another
important moment in the development of a political
tradition which was to become the property of all parties in England as they achieved responsibility and power. It is the main theme of the second half of the present
book.

In 1944 Sir Ernest Barker asked me to combine my
study of theses two topics and adjust them to the purposes of his "Current Problems" series. After twenty-
five years, the result of this strikes me as comic, and I
have kept the contemporary allusions as they originally
stood, so that, in this aspect, the work shall be clearly a
museum piece. If I were writing at the present day I
would lay greater stress on the phrase (p. 108): "we may
be too enslaved to the past, lacking the elasticity of mind
that is necessary to meet the demands of a rapidly changing world". I do not suppose that I differ from the
rebellious young in my judgment of present-day society.
I differ from them in my feeling that by our wilfulness
we can easily make things worse. If there are apostles
of "apocalyptic politics" in the world today, I should
regard the fundamental argument of the present book as
still relevant therfore. I may perhaps add that the subject
of the first half of this book is treated more definitely
from the technical historian's point of view in my Sten-
ton Lecture: *Magna Carta in the Historiography of the
Sixteenth and Seventeenth Centuries* (Reading, 1969).
The subject of the second half is treated from a differ-

ent angle in my "Oration" at the London School of Economics and Politics, *History as the Emancipation from the Past* (London, 1956).

H.B.

September 1969

INTRODUCTION

In the crisis of 1940 our leaders continually reminded us of those resources in the past which can be drawn upon to fortify a nation at war. While plunging into a sea of changes, novelties and inventions, England resumed contact with her traditions and threw out ropes to the preceding generations, as though in time of danger it was a good thing not to lose touch with the rest of the convoy. It may seem strange that, though the past is over, it is at the same time here—something of it still remaining, alive and momentous for us. But the past, like the spent part of a cinematograph film, is coiled up inside the present. It is part of the very structure of the 20th-century world.

Some nations have had a broken and tragic past. Others are new or have only recently arisen after a long submergence. Some have been torn by a terrible breach between past and present—a breach which, though it happened long ago, they have never been able to heal and overcome. We in England have been fortunate and we must remember our good fortune, for we have actually drawn strength from the continuity of our history. We have been wise, for we have taken care of the processes which serve to knit the past and the present together; and when great rifts have occurred—in the Reformation or the Civil Wars, for example—a succeeding generation has done its best to play providence upon the tears and rents that have been made in the fabric of our history. Englishmen in the after-period have actually thrown back the needle, seeking by a thousand little stitches to join the present with the past once more. So we are a country of traditions and there remains a living continuity in our history.

It is our object to study the relations of Englishmen with their history and the means by which the past and the present have been kept in alliance; also to take stock of some of the riches that have been ours as a result of this alliance, this preservation of the silt of bygone centuries in the fabric of the present day. We shall concern ourselves not with the conservatism that resists all changes, not with any passion to preserve the past just as it "really was"; but rather with the methods by which continuity has been reconciled with change, and the past has been used to assist our purposes. We shall study the working of these methods in what may be described as the great formative period, when our political traditions were taking the shape that we recognize to-day; when Englishmen developed their characteristic attitude to their own history—developed that "whig interpretation" which was never more vivid than in the great speeches of 1940. We shall observe something of the rôle which this traditional interpretation has played in English politics and progress—in the acquisition of our liberties. Then we shall examine some of the other factors that have helped to make this country strong in its political traditions; so that we may see how even in the practice of politics Englishmen acquired and handed down from one generation to another a characteristic method and policy—a system which we can call our own.

Studying these things, we can hardly help commemorating those whigs of the past who were always so much greater than the whig historians. We shall see how they evolved an attitude to the historical process, a way of co-operating with the forces of history, an alliance with Providence, which the whig historians were much slower to achieve— which they were even perhaps too partisan to discern. We shall see how this, too, became the common heritage of Englishmen—how the services of the whigs (like the influence of Shakespeare on English life) are things which pass, so to speak, into a conjuror's hat, precisely because they become the property of all, the heritage of both whig and tory; with the result that when we speak of England's contribution to the art of politics and the machinery of government, we do not always remember how much they are the gift of the whigs—partisan at first perhaps, but later qualified, and finally absorbed into a tradition that is nation-wide.

H. B.

February 1944

CONTENTS

PART II: THE POLITICAL TRADITION

PART I: THE HISTORY

ↄ

I. THE ENGLISHMAN AND HIS HISTORY

The English Tradition in Historical Interpretation

ALTHOUGH history may often seem to be—like the natural sciences—an international study, transcending racial and political frontiers, its interpretation remains more profoundly national, more stubbornly local, than many of us realize or perhaps trouble to keep in mind. We may imagine that here in England we are free from the prejudices and enthusiasms of other nations. Sometimes we think that our history is the impartial narrative, and we hardly believe that we are performing an act of interpretation at all. But however much we refine and elaborate, it is not clear that we reach—or that without great intellectual endeavour we could hope to reach—more than the English view of Louis XIV. And our best biography of Napoleon is only the supreme expression of what is really the English version of the man's career. We teach and write the kind of history which is appropriate to our organization, congenial to the intellectual climate of our part of the world. We can scarcely help it if this kind of history is at the same time the one most adapted to the preservation of the existing regime.

Our initial object is to study the so-called whig

interpretation of history, as an aspect of the English mind and as a product of the English tradition. We shall treat it not as a thing invented by some particularly wilful historian, but as part of the landscape of English life, like our country lanes or our November mists or our historic inns. Along with the English language and the British constitution and our national genius for compromise, it is itself a product of history, part of the inescapable inheritance of Englishmen. We can say that it moulded Englishmen before anybody moulded it or began to be conscious of it at all.

One man in the 18th century wrote essays on English history so full of the song of liberty that he has been called the founder of the whig interpretation; yet he was none other than the politician Bolingbroke, notorious in his day and ever since as the wildest and wickedest of tories. The tories in fact do not escape the whig interpretation, though they may try to undermine it and they play tricks with it at times—they attempt for example to show that on occasion they themselves, rather than the whigs, were the real promotors of our present-day liberty. And there is not anything in England worth considering on the other side—there is not anything worth the name of "the tory interpretation of English history". It is really the "English" interpretation that we are discussing therefore, and from the way in which it developed we may see that it is like the British constitution—itself the product of history and vicissitude. It provided the most obvious method by which Englishmen could make capital out of their own past and put the history of earlier centuries to practical use. It represented indeed the way in which Englishmen would naturally view their past in days when the historical sense had not been tuned and trained. Great originality of mind would have been required in Englishmen to enable them to escape the whig interpretation. And it has needed generations of historical research to make us understand how closely our forefathers were the prisoners of it.

Those who, amid the breeze and agitation of contemporary debate, affect to court a controversy with such diluted remnants of the whig interpretation as still keep their currency amongst us, must take heed when they sally forth in their carpet slippers against this entrenched tradition. They will find a more comfortable piece of coast for their commandos if they will carry their offensive, not against the whig tradition itself, but against surviving defects in historical method. It is not necessary or useful to deny that the theme of English political history is the story of our liberty; and while men think that freedom is worth singing songs about, from New York to Cape Town, from London to Canberra, it will always be true that in one important respect—in yesterday's meaning of the term at least—we are all of us exultant and unrepentant whigs. Those who, perhaps in the misguided austerity of youth, wish to drive out that whig interpretation, (that particular thesis which controls our abridgment of English history,) are sweeping a room which humanly speaking cannot long remain empty. They are opening the door for seven devils which, precisely because they are new-comers, are bound to be worse than the first.

We, on the other hand, will not dream of wishing it away, but will rejoice in an interpretation of the past which has grown up with us, has grown up with the history itself, and has helped to make the history. New interpretations always come with crudeness and violence at first, as we shall see. They erupt upon the world as propaganda; they must make their way as fighting creeds. They can become wise and urbane, perhaps even harmless, all of them, but only after they have submitted to the chastening effect of controversy, discipline and tradition. Therefore, though we seek to tear it asunder, and to make clear what we may call the mere mechanics of its rise and its operation, we will celebrate this whig inheritance of ours with a robust but regulated pride; observing the part which an interpretation of history has played in building up the centuries and creating the England that we know.

The Englishman's Alliance with his History

Although it might seem strange to us to-day that Macaulay should ever have imagined his *History of England* as transcending party prejudice, he gives almost at the opening of that work an explanation of whig and tory partisanship in the treatment of his-torical problems. His account seems to beg the essential question, but it must be mentioned since it raises a matter of genuine interest. It is a useful introduction to an enquiry into the origin of the whig interpretation.

Macaulay refers to the fact that England has always taken particular pride in the maintenance of her institutional continuity. Our statesmen and lawyers have been under the influence of the past to a greater degree than those of other countries. From the 17th century our greatest innovators have tried to show that they were not innovators at all but restorers of ancient ways. And so it is that even when we have a revolution we look to the past and try to carry it out in accordance with ancient precedents. It is different in France as Macaulay explains—different especially since the Revolution of 1789. A Frenchman has no need to exaggerate the power of Louis XIV or underrate the ancient rights of the Parlement of Paris. He can take the view that the year 1789 rules a line across the story, he can say that modern France has a new start at the Revolution; while in modern England, if an unusual problem arises, the procedure may have to be determined upon precedents that go back to the middle ages. So in all English controversies both parties have referred to history in order to discover what they wished to discover—both parties have had a colossal vested interest in the historical enquiries that were taking place.

That marriage between the present and the past which Macaulay describes has been an interesting feature of English life, English law and English politics—a side of our story rich with latent values, and a restful thing for the mind to reflect upon. We have maintained a curious respect for law sometimes, even in periods of severe internal stress. In periods of change we have learned not to rush heedlessly onwards but to walk with a due regard for precedent. Yet this respect for the past has been combined with (perhaps even it has been dependent on) what one might call a sublime and purposeful unhistoricity. We have not in fact—however sincere our illusions on the subject—been the slaves and the prisoners of the "genuine antique", the dead hand of archaic custom. And if we have clung to the past it has been to a nicely chosen past—one which was conveniently and tidily disposed for our purposes.

In particular we must congratulate ourselves that our 17th-century forefathers, for all their antiquarian fervour, did not resurrect and fasten upon us the authentic middle ages. Those "historic rights" to which Englishmen (especially in the Stuart period) so loved to appeal—it was essential that they should not have been rigid, but should have moved with the centuries, that "ancient custom" should have been a living thing, to save us from the pressure of a fossilized antiquity. The good terms that Englishmen have managed to keep with their own bygone centuries have been the counterpart of their ability to make the past move with them, so to speak. They have depended on the ability of our 17th-century ancestors to see the middle ages not—if one may use the phrase—"as they really were", but in terms that were appropriate to the Stuart age.

The French were different. When in the *Fronde*, in the middle of the 17th century, they asserted "historic rights" and "ancient custom" against the king, it was a genuine piece of history, a genuine survival from the past, that reared itself up against the monarchy. In France there still existed over-mighty subjects, semi-feudal potentates, privileged corporations—all clinging to private rights that were rooted in a continuous tradition. And the French, having been too much the slaves of their own preceding centuries, set out to free themselves in 1789—they ended in fact by cursing their middle ages and repudiating their past. French liberty springs from a revolt against history and tradition—a revolt that suffered a serious handicap because it was based on the abstract "rights of man". But in England we made peace with our middle ages by misconstruing them; and, therefore, we may say that "wrong" history was one of our assets. The whig interpretation came at exactly the crucial moment and, whatever it may have done to our history, it had a wonderful effect on English politics. For this reason England did not need a revolution of 1789 to save her from the despotism of the past. We did not need to resort to abstract philosophy—our liberty is based on "the historic rights of Englishmen". We did not have to demolish a tradition which stood rigid like a wall, hindering the transmutation of custom. And though we did have a revolution in the 17th century it did not make us "happy ever afterwards"—it only taught us to treasure more dearly the continuity of our history. We hastened to tie up the threads and re-constitute the customs which linked the past with the present. And consciously we seem to have deter-mined never to let such an aberration take place again.

But, for this marriage between "progress" and "tradition" in the English story, the rôle of the Tudors was an absolute necessity. It is important that there was a period in English history when all the loyalty of the country was centred upon the monarch. We seemed to forget in the 16th century those "ancient rights" which had once been asserted against the crown. If indeed those historic rights and traditional privileges were remembered at all, they were recognized to have been reactionary, aristocratic and dangerous, as we shall see. The Tudors, we may say, performed for England much of the work which the French Revolution achieved for France. It was they who represented the breach with the past and who liquidated those things in the middle ages which men were delighted to be parted from. Under the Tudors we see the end of the feudal epoch, the rise of the middle class to political signifi-cance, and the realization of "the idea of the state". And it was the Tudors who imposed upon the people a notion of public policy that transcended the older concepts of private rights. It was we in England who, in the 16th century, did not care even to remem-ber the regime of private rights and feudal assertive-ness out of which we had too recently emerged. We worshiped our Tudor monarchs precisely because they had repressed this kind of abuse.

And so, the notion of historic rights, forgotten for a time under the Tudors, had to be recaptured —as something lost awhile—by historical enquiry; and it came to its full blossoming in the historiography of the early 17th century. Historic rights had to be summoned to new life again, not, as in France, by semi-feudal potentates whose claims had a continuous tradition behind them, but by middle-class citizens interested in antiquarian research. And when they emerged they had not the flavour of the *ancien régime*—they did not appear as a reassertion of reactionary feudal privilege at all. Indeed it is quite a question whether the rights that were put forward in the 17th century were genuinely "historical" in the sense we should give to the word. A conception of customary rights which had been the privilege and the glory of an aristocracy was taken over by the middle classes. Ancient "liberties" became generalized in the process and were transmuted into modern "liberty". Rights that had once been inimical to the central government were harnessed and subdued to the idea of the state. Feudal limitations on the royal power were called to mind again in a world that knew not the historic feudalism, and they were curiously reconstrued. All the changes that had taken place in the order of society gave even the old terminology new implications and new power. And, precisely because they did not know the middle ages, the historians of the time gave the 17th century just the type of anachronism that it required. Roughly speaking, we may say that only after 1600 do the worship of *Magna Carta* (as the charter of middle-class freedom), the superstition for historic rights, and the whig interpretation of history, come into effective existence after the curious interval afforded by the Tudor period. All three were born out of the same complex of events and conditions. They are joint products of one live piece of history.

The necessary background to the history of the rise of the whig interpretation, then, is that Tudor period in which the common Englishman knew no better than to be thankful for his kings. It was a period in which the recent victory of the national monarchy would appear as the culmination, indeed the end, of whatever historical process men were conscious of. We start therefore with an extreme tory interpretation—one not darkly hinted at, but distinctly formulated by the writers of histories. We need not shudder at the thought that this, too, was proper in its time and place—was so to speak organic to the age itself. It represented something like the meaning of the history, as this had been unfolded up to date.

It is typical of the English that, retaining what was a good in the past, but reconstruing it—reconstruing the past itself if necessary—they have clung to the monarchy, and have maintained it down to the present, while changing its import and robbing it of the power to do harm. It is typical of them that from their 17th-century revolution itself and from the very experiment of an interregnum, they learned

that there was still a subtle utility in kingship and
they determined to reconstitute their traditions again,
lest they should throw away the good with the bad.
In all this there is something more profound than a
mere sentimental unwillingness to part with a piece
of ancient pageantry—a mere disinclination to sacrifice the ornament of a royal court. Here we have a
token of that alliance of Englishmen with their history which has prevented the uprooting of things that
have been organic to the development of the country;
which has enriched our institutions with echoes and
overtones; and which has proved—against the presumption and recklessness of blind revolutionary
overthrows—the happier form of co-operation with
Providence.

II. THE TUDOR PERIOD

The Development of Tudor Historical Writing

IN the 16th century we see the explicit formulation of what we must call the tory interpretation of English history.

The historical writing of the early Tudor period is rude and rustic—often a mere compilation or "Abridgment" of the medieval chroniclers. Such annals, even in Elizabeth's reign, would start with the Creation, and famous historians late in the century could repeat the legend that the Britons were descended from the Trojans, though they might state that its truth had been challenged. Remarks about the weather at some remarkable season, and tales of prodigies and portents in certain years, would interrupt the narrative of wars, rebellions and dynastic intrigues.

A foreigner, Polydore Vergil, introduced a more critical attitude to the chroniclers in the early 16th century, but his views were sometimes attributed to his jealousy as a foreigner, and Bishop John Bale, while admitting the extent of Vergil's learning, charged him with deforming his writings greatly, "polluting our English Chronicles most shamefully with his Romish lies and other Italish beggarys". Bale adds:

I would wish some learned Englishman (as there are now most excellent fresh wits) to set forth the

English Chronicles in their right shape, as certain
other lands have done afore them, all affections set
apart. I cannot think a more necessary thing to be
laboured to the honour of God, beauty of the realm,
erudition of the people, and commodity of other
lands, next the sacred scriptures of the Bible, than
that work would be.

Bale, a passionate Protestant, was greatly concerned
for English historiography, anxious for the preservation and the printing of ancient chronicles, of which
he set out to compile a register. He was not too blind
to see the deficiencies of his own nation in this
matter, and deplored that "our Chronycles" were
"by fabulous wryters sore blemyshed". He was the
friend of Leland, and in spite of the violence of his
Protestant feeling, in spite of the virulence of his
hatred of monks, he deplored the destruction of
books and manuscripts which attended the dissolu-
tion of the monasteries.

Amonge all the nacions in whome I have wan-
dered, for the knowledge of thynges . . . I haue
founde nene so negligent and vntoward, as I haue
found England in the due serch of theyr auncyent
hystoryes, to the syngulare fame and bewyte thereof.
. . . A much forther plage hath fallen of late yeares
I dolorouslye lamente so great an oversyghte in
the moste lawfull ouerthrow of the sodometrouse
Abbeyes and Fryeries, when the most worthy monumentes of this realme, so myserably peryshed in the
spoyle. . . .
I iudge thys to be true, and vtter it wyth heavy-
nesse, that neyther the Brytanes vnder the Romanes
and Saxons, nor yet the Englyshe people vndre the

Danes and Normannes, had euer such dammage of their lerned monumentes, as we have seane in our time.

"Bilious Bale", as he was called, was associated with Matthew Parker in attempts to secure such monastic manuscripts as could be rescued after the middle of the century.

It is clear that Englishmen were not entirely satisfied with the condition of historical study as the 16th century proceeded ; and if on the one hand the Reformation helped to produce a reaction against the monkish chroniclers, on the other hand the influences of the Italian Renaissance brought a more profound appreciation of the meaning of history. The introduction to Cooper's *Abridgement of the Chronicles* repeats Machiavelli's teaching that history can be an education for political leaders, since the problems of statesmanship always remain essentially the same. The examples from the past may serve as a pattern for rulers, therefore, just in the way that models are used in the plastic arts. Some writers stress the analogy between one period and another, and regard one age as the "mirror" of another age, just as a lawyer might go to the minority of Henry III for precedents that would be applicable to the case of Edward VI. Sir Walter Ralegh at the end of the century sees successive cycles, repetitions of pattern, in the course of world history.

The Tudor attitude to history is well exemplified in a curious volume, with the significant title *A Mirror for Magistrates*, which first appeared just after the middle of the century and which proved to be one of the popular works of the English Renaissance. It consisted of a series of verse narratives, which came out with successive enlargements in later editions; but in spite of its curious form—and in spite of some brilliant poetry that it contains—it has been described as

the first important work which released English history from the chronicles and employed it directly for the purposes accepted as the ends to be achieved by history, using the freedom of poetry to adapt its means more directly to the ends to be served.

It was a composite work, and, (since lawyers have an important place in the whole course of development that we have to study,) it is relevant to note that some of its promoters were lawyers, and one of the contributors, George Ferrers, had translated *Magna Carta* into English. It was based on a collection of narratives by Boccaccio, (translated into English as *The Fall of Princes,*) and it described the downfall of various magnates in English history—holding the mirror of the past up to the present so that the appropriate lesson would emerge. It contained some interesting lines on the importance of "causes" in history:

> Unfruytful Fabyan folowed the face
> Of time and dedes, but let the causes slip. . . .
>
> But seeing causes are the chiefest things
> That should be noted of the story wryters
> That men may learne what endes al causes bringes

> They be unworthy the name of Chroniclers
> That leaue these cleane out of their registers
> Or doubtfully report them.

Grafton, in the Dedicatory Letter prefixed to his *Chronicle* (1568), illustrates the transition from the "Chronicle" stage. He says of earlier historians that some of them, "meaning to write short notes in the maner of Annales, commonly called Abridgements, rather touch the tymes when things were done, than declare the maner of the doyngs, leauing thereby some necessitie of larger explication".

Moving beyond the mere chronicle of events, history becomes the study of causes, the source of parallelisms and lessons, and the vehicle of propaganda. Such a development in its early years is seldom "pure" or austerely disciplined—the scholarly interest merges with other preoccupations (the desire to arouse patriotic enthusiasm for example) and the learning is not unperverted by passion or unbiassed by the affections. Austere standards in this respect do not come from the mere personal sincerity and moral rectitude of the individual historian—they are things which can hardly be achieved without long training, without the chastening effects of tradition and criticism.

Apart from the technical views current in the Tudor age on the subject of the functions of historical writers, therefore, we have to study the basic prejudices which governed the moralizings of the historians and guided the course of the enquiry that was pursued. One of the primary motives of historians in the 16th century does not concern us just now, and therefore it may merely be mentioned in passing—it was the desire to support the cause of the Lancastrians and to glorify the victory of the house of Tudor. Another passion which was the motor of much historical activity was the enthusiasm for the cause of the Reformation in England. In an Introduction to Grafton's *Chronicle* we are told in the usual way what are the lessons we shall draw if we trouble to read the ensuing narrative. One of the chief points is: that the Ecclesiastical State will learn "to abhorre trayterous practices and indignities done against Kings". Grafton's History is in fact a gigantic piece of anti-Catholic propaganda. Fabyan's Chronicle was written before the Reformation but further editions appeared afterwards, in 1542 and 1549. In these later editions a multitude of pious references and stories of saints were tactfully omitted and the glorification of Thomas à Becket was left out. Becket was the centre of one of those sections of the English story that had to be recast after the Reformation. Henceforward, everything had to be in praise of kings.

The *Mirror for Magistrates* (both in its verse narratives and in the prose expositions that are the prelude to the stories) summarizes the political teaching put forward by the Tudor historians generally and sometimes expounded in the introductions to their works. It was always assumed that kings held their power from God, and especially in their capacity as the dispensers of justice they were to be regarded as standing in the place of God. Kings, however, were held to be responsible to God, and in these days when faith was still a vivid thing the words were not taken as implying "responsible to nobody on earth", but involved the view that kings would be called to account for their conduct—that it was incumbent upon them to rule in accordance with some sort of law. In particular those kings who were capricious in their government would be punished by God either in this world or in the next. Subjects, however, must always be submissive to their kings and never rebel, even against the wicked ones. They must regard even tyrannical and capricious monarchs as they would regard bad weather or a famine—as a chastisement from God. God may use rebels in order to punish a tyrannical king as He once used godless tribes to punish even His chosen people of Israel. Still He does not approve of rebels and it is always wicked to rebel. Those who resort to force may do some harm to the king, but they will do no good to the state and after all their violence they will not be any better off themselves. Even though the king is wicked it is necessary to leave the retribution to God.

This set of ideas, embedded in the very fabric of Tudor historical writing, is the tory and Church of England doctrine of non-resistance which flourished down to 1688 and even survived the Revolution for a time. As an interpretation of history it is somewhat forced; the political teaching is by no means married to the narrative itself in the work of the Tudor writers. Having learned that their study should issue in political lessons, these authors—their theory ahead of their practice—naturally discover the lessons which they already know to be right.

Even under a strong monarchy, however, a people will hardly consent to sing songs in favour of slavery. The supporters of the Tudors (Ralegh for example) could compliment the monarchs on being rulers of free-men rather than masters of slaves. The *Mirror for Magistrates* condemns arbitrary government and shows the fate that attends the unjust judge. It contains a curious series of verses entitled "Howe Collingbourne was cruelly executed for making a foolishe rime", where we are told that the poet who has attacked a tyrant must "gallop thence to kepe his carkas safe". In the prose commentary on this poem the moral is even applied to the 16th century:

Gods blessing on his heart that made thys (sayd one) specially for reuiuinge our auncient liberties. And pray God it may take suche place with the Magistrates, that they maye ratifie an olde freedome.

The Tudor Glorification of King John

If all these things are kept in mind—the Protestant fervour of Tudor historians, the reaction against monastic chroniclers, the adoration of monarchy, the hatred of rebellion even though it might be against a wicked tyrant—we shall be in a better position to understand the Tudor attitude to King John. And if we remember the way in which one reign can be made to seem the parallel or the mirror of another reign, we can appreciate why the reign of John could be regarded as a counterpart to that of Henry VIII.

One of the interesting Tudor plays before the time of Shakespeare is a work entitled *King John*, associated with the John Bale who has already been mentioned as a virulent Protestant and a keen lover of history. It is not concerned with *Magna Carta* in any way—the whole play is in fact a glorification of monarchy. John is the hero, the patriot, the "morning star of the Reformation". He is the precursor of Henry VIII because of the magnitude of his conflict with the papacy. Standing half-way between the miracle play and the historical drama of Shakespeare's time, the work, which belongs to the middle of the century, contains allegorical figures like Sedition, Private Wealth, Usurped Power, Dissimulation. But these abstract figures tend to turn into historical characters —Sedition is Stephen Langton and Usurped Power turns into the Pope. There is a summing-up by "Interpretatour" at the close of Act I and this passage illustrates the tone of the whole work:

In thys present acte we have to you declared,
As in a myrrour, the begynnynge of Kynge Johan,
How he was of God a magistrate appoynted
To the governaunce of thys same noble regyon,
To see mayntayned the true faythe and relygyon;
But Satan the Devyll, which that time was at large,
Had so great a swaye that he coulde it not dis-
        charge. . . .
This noble Kynge Johan, as a faythfull Moses
Withstode proude Pharao for hys poore Israel,

> Myndyng to brynge yt owt of the lande of darke-
>   nesse, [i.e. papistry].
> But the Egyptyanes did agaynst hym so rebell,
> That hys poore people ded styll in the desart
>   dwell,
> Tyll that duke Josue, whych was our late Kynge
>   Henrye,
> Clerely brought us in to the lande of mylke and
>   honye.

Towards the end of Act II "Veryte" enlarges on the
good deeds of King John and talks of the untruths
which historians have spread concerning him. At
one point John is described as a Lollard. In his fare-
well to England he is made to say, "I am ryght sorye
I coulde do for the[e] no more". Great advantage
is taken of the fact that in this reign the pope
fomented sedition against the king, as he was doing
in the Tudor period. In a quite different work, *A
Supplication for the Beggars* (1529), the same point
appears and Henry VIII has to listen to a reference
to "your illustrious predecessor, King John". Some
Tudor writers, (Grafton for example,) manage to
heighten the dramatic effect by pointing out that the
pope whom John resisted was Innocent III, in whom
the papacy reached the summit of its arrogance; and
that these were the days when auricular confession
and the doctrine of transubstantiation were imposed
upon the world.

An early chronicle play, printed in 1591, was
The Troublesome Raigne of Iohn King of England.
It has an introduction addressed "to the Gentlemen
Readers":

You that with friendly grace of smoothed brow
Haue entertained the Scythian Tamburlane,
And given applause vnto an infidel:
Vouchsafe to welcome (with like curtesie)
A warlike Christian and your Countryman.
For Christ's true faith indurr'd he many a storme,
And set himselfe against the Man of Rome,
Vntill base treason (by a damned wight)
Did all his former triumphs put to flight.
Accept of it (sweet Gentles) in good sort
And thinke it was preparde for your disport.

Many passages show that the writer has Henry VIII
and the Tudors in mind—as when John is made to
say "Never an Italian Priest of them all shal either
haue tithe, tole or polling pennie out of England;
but as I am King, so will I raigne next under God".
A remarkable speech, in which John justifies himself
as the despoiler of monasteries, begins

Ile ceaze the lasie Abbey lubbers lands
Into my hands to pay my men of warre.

Rebellion is denounced, even when "the wrongs are
true", and the pope is condemned as the instigator
of rebels. John finally says:

My tongue doth falter: Philip, I tell thee man:
Since Iohn did yeeld vnto the Priest of Rome,
Nor he nor his haue prospred on the earth:
Curst are his blessings, and his curse is blisse
But in the spirit I cry vnto my God,
As did the Kingly Prophet David cry,
(Whose hands, as mine with murder were attaint.)
I am not he shall build the Lord a house,
Or root these locusts from the face of earth:
But if my dying heart deceive me not,

From out these loynes shall spring a kingly braunch
Whose armes shall reach vnto the gates of Rome,
And with his feete tread downe the Strumpets
    pride
That sits upon the Chaire of Babylon.

In 1611, Speed still gave the Reformation account of King John, described him as the victim of clerical spite, and closed with the following verdict: "Whose Raigne had it not fallen in the time of so turbulent a' *Pope*, so ambitious Neighbour *Princes*, so disloyall Subiects, nor his Story into the hands of exasperated Writers, he had appeared a King of as great renowne, as misfortunes".[1]

The compiler Grafton is evidently responsible for much of the enthusiasm shown by the author of *The Troublesome Raigne*. Grafton stresses the ecclesiastical causes of the disturbances in the time of John, whom, he says, men "ought to haue obeyed though he had bene euill, euen for very conscience sake". Fabyan's pre-Reformation (1516) verdict had been very unfavourable to John; but it is not without significance that it was omitted from the post-Reformation editions of 1542 and 1549.

The attempt to rehabilitate King John perhaps

---

[1] Speed wrote of the dissensions of this reign as follows: ". . . Which certaine miseries, and vncertaine sydings in *ciuill warres* are not so strange, as is the savage madnesse of disloyall dispositions, who to attaine a shadow of *seeming Liberties* immerge themselues and their abettors into bottomlesse seruitudes and distresses. . . . Many likewise were the grievances into which the Barons the mean while were plunged; to see their Native Country by their own wilfulness thus horribly massacred."

never quite succeeded, and it seems to have been confined to the crucial periods when papal authority was the subject of direct attack. John's popularity seems to wane towards the end of the century in any case, and in Shakespeare he is neither the hero nor the villain, though he has moments of majesty. One of the crimes imputed to him was calculated to move even Tudor writers against him—for the Tudors attached importance to the legitimacy of kings and to the principle of primogeniture. It was admitted that the death of Arthur, if John was responsible for it, was a reprehensible crime. After the death of Arthur, however, John was the legitimate king, and whatever his sins—whatever their private grievances—the nobles were unjustified in their rebellion against him.

In Shakespeare (who takes much of his material from *The Troublesome Raigne*) the conflict with France, the relations with the pope, the problem of Arthur, and the rebellions of the nobles are the chief themes in the play. John is not the murderer of Arthur, though he almost allows himself to become the instigator of the crime—he gives a hint that he desires the boy's death, but repents later as though recovering from a momentary evil impulse. Pandulph says, "Blessed shall he be that doth revolt"; but the lords, having rebelled, return to their obedience, when they are convinced that their French ally is going to betray them—is indeed only making use of them to bring about the fall of John. At this point Salisbury says:

But I do love the favour and the form
Of this most fair occasion, by the which
We will untread the steps of damned flight,
And like a bated and retired flood,
Leaving our rankness and irregular course,
Stoop low within those bounds we have o'erlook'd
And calmly run on in obedience,
Even to our ocean, to our great King John.

Magna Carta *in the Tudor Period*

Though some pre-Reformation writers refer to it,
the Great Charter had an insignificant place in Tudor
historical writing until towards the close of the
century. No mention of it is to be found in the three
plays which have been referred to above. Cooper's
Chronicle (1560) does not speak of it, though under
the year 1216 we are told that John "would not use
the lawes of St. Edward and other auncient liberties".
Cooper says that the nobles "mainteyned a warre
against King John to the great hurt of this realme of
England". John Harding's verse chronicle contains
no mention of the Charter. Grafton makes no reference to the grant of *Magna Carta*, but under the
year 1212 he describes how the pope tore up "the
Great Charter of the liberties of England".

Speed in 1611, writing of *Magna Carta*, said:

Thus one of the greatest *souereigns* of *Christendome*,
was now become the *twenty sixt petty King in his owne
Dominions*. . . . What maruaille if high disdain hereof
pierced his swelling heart and filled his minde with
reuoluing thoughts, how to vnwinde himselfe of
those seruile fetters?

Magna Carta was first published by Richard Pynson in 1499. It was translated in the middle of the 16th century by George Ferrers. Particularly after the middle of the century the publication of the Statutes of the Realm became common, and the Great Charter was always given as the first of the statutes. In all these cases, however, it was the reissue of 9 Henry III which was printed; and even when Sir Edward Coke wrote his famous commentary on the Charter, it was a commentary on the Charter of Henry III, though Coke in a footnote declared that there had also been a Charter in John's reign and that it, too, had been called *Magna Carta*.[1] In about the year 1610 Selden printed a version of the *Magna Carta* of King John, using the chronicle of Matthew Paris. Spelman, in his work *Of Parliaments*, quotes part of the Charter of John on the authority of Matthew Paris together with the Red Book of the Exchequer. In 1650, however, J. Jones published the Charter of Henry III separately, stating

[1] Cowell's *Interpreter*, published in 1637, has a passage which runs as follows: "*Magna Charta*, called in English the great charter, is a charter conteining a number of lawes ordeined the ninth yeare of *Henry* the third, and confirmed by *Edward* the first. The reason why it was tearmed *Magna Charta*, was either that it conteined the summe of all the written lawes in England, or else that there was another Charter called the Charter of the Forest, established with it, which in quantitie was the lesser of the two. I read *in Holinshed*, that King *Iohn*, to appease his Barons, yelded to lawes, or articles of government, much like to this great Charter; but wee nowe haue noe auncienter writen lawe, then this, which was thought to be so beneficall to the subiect . . . that K. *Henry* the third was thought but hardly to yeld vnto it."

that the full volume of Statutes was too voluminous and costly for the generality to read or buy. *A Declaration of the Liberties of the English Nation* 1681 says that "*Magna Charta* and *Charta de Foresta*, being both made in 9 Henry III and confirmed Edward I do in effect treat of the same matter and therefore both are called the Great Charters of the Liberties of England". Copies of John's Charter were beginning to be brought to light in the 17th century. One was presented by Mr. Humphrey Wyem to Cotton in 1628. Another, found at Dover Castle, was given to Cotton by the Warden, Sir Edward Dering, in 1630. There was a fable that Cotton discovered this latter copy by accident in a London tailor's shop. The Salisbury Cathedral copy was known at the close of the 17th century, but important historical writers were unaware of the existence of any of the four originals. William Nicholson, writing in 1699, said, "we have not one copy of this inestimable piece". McKechnie states that the actual Charter of John was not printed until the time of Blackstone and that prior to this date, 1759, "even the best informed writers on English history laboured under much confusion. . . . Few seem to have been aware that fundamental differences existed between the Charter granted by John and the reissue of Henry III."[1]

---

[1] Bémont mentions that French historians (e.g. A. Duchesne, *Histoire générale d'Angleterre*, 1614) had no reference to *Magna Carta*. "Le P. d'Orléans paraît être le premier à parler chez nous de cet acte" (i.e. in the *Histoire des révolutions d'Angleterre*

This being the case, it will be relevant to discover
what the Tudor writers had to say about the Great
Charter in the reign of Henry III. Some indeed pass
over the year 9 Henry III without mentioning it;
others refer to it without comment or dismiss it
briefly as a merely feudal document, having reference
to questions like "wardship and marriage". Rastell,
The Pasture of the People (1529), says:

About the VIII yere of this kynges reyne, the
charter called Magna Carta was cōfyrmed, and dyuers
artycles addyd therto, howe the kynge shulde haue
the warde and maryage of the lordes heyres beynge
within age, and the first statute of Mortmayne than
made. . . .

Cooper's *Chronicle* (1560) says under the year 1225:

The Lordes and Gentilmen of England fyrst
granted to Kyng Henrie the warde and mariage of
theyr heyres.[1]

depuis le commencement de la monarchie, 3 vols. Paris, 1693). Rapin
in 1728 published a French translation of *Magna Carta* and the
Charter of the Forest, in his history.

[1] Arthur Hall (1575) mentions John's Charter, and then
writes of Henry III, "At the motion of the Archbishoppe of
Caunterbury and others the Lordes, the King [9 Henry III]
graunted and confirmed the greate Charter; thereupon (as I
can gather by some records) the warde and mariage of our
children was graunted to the King". Grafton says that in
1218 "King Edward's laws were again restored and *Magna
Carta* confirmed", and that in 1223 "the Barony in Parliament
Graunted to the King and his successors warde and marriage
of their heyres"—which grant is the object of his bitter indignation. Fabyan, who mentions neither the Charter nor King
Edward's laws in the reign of Henry III, attacks the grant of
wardship and marriage "which dede was after of lernyed men
called iniciũ malarum, that is to mene, the begynning of illes
or harmes".

Magna Carta did not save England from the despotism of the Tudors. A generation which glorified the monarchy, deprecated rebellion even against tyrants, and regarded the nobility as the source of faction, was not likely to make great use of historic rights against its beloved Tudor monarchs—men did not wish to be rescued from their kings. Sometimes a chronicler will mention a confirmation of the Charter of the Forest without a word about the confirmation of *Magna Carta* at the same time. But the truth was that these historians were casual compilers or they were Protestant propagandists; and Pullen was right in his judgment of contemporary historians when he said that chroniclers were occupied with wars while the lawyers made a profounder study of law and government. A book of Statutes in the 1540's spoke of the "Great Chartour . . . graunted to all the cominalte of the realme"; and showed how it had had "to be red foure tymes in the yere before the people in the full countye" and how an episcopal curse had been put upon all breakers of it. But volumes of statutes were not for the common reader. And there is no sign that *Magna Carta* was regarded as a live affair.

In 1550 we first hear of a document called the *Mirror of Justice* which became famous at a later date because of the tricks that it played upon English historical writing. It was circulated in manuscript amongst lawyers after 1550, was printed in 1642 and was translated into English in 1648. Coke believed that it set forth the full law of King Arthur's day, and his final opinion put it before the Norman

Conquest, though he had to recognize that there
had been later additions. Chapter V, Section 2 of this
work is on "The defects of the Great Charter" and
its circulation in the latter part of the 16th century is
perhaps the first sign of the movement that we have
to examine. It states that "the Law of this Realm
founded upon 40 points of the Great Charter of
Liberties is damnably dis-used by the Governours
of the Law and by Statutes afterwards made contrary to some of the points". It calls particular
attention to the clause of *Magna Carta* which says
that the king shall "not disseise, nor imprison nor
destroy, but by lawfull ijdgement". It showed how
this clause was being contravened in various ways
—for example, by imprisonment for debt—and how
even certain of our statutes were of no validity
because they were inconsistent with it. We shall see
that it was this clause which in the subsequent period
did most to draw attention to the whole problem
of *Magna Carta*.

III. THE FOUNDERS OF THE WHIG
INTERPRETATION

The Rise of a New Historical Movement

IN the reign of Elizabeth there began to emerge a remarkable interest in historical studies and in 1572 a Society of Antiquaries was formed. Sir Henry Spelman's *Original of the Four Terms of the Year*, (written in 1614), begins:

About forty-two Years since, divers Gentlemen in London, studious of Antiquities, formed themselves into a College or Society of Antiquaries, appointing to meet every Friday weekly in the Term, at a place agreed of, and for Learning sake to confer upon some Question in that Faculty and to sup together. The Place, after a Meeting or two became certain at . . . the Herald's Office . . . and two Questions were propounded at every Meeting to be handled at the next that followed. . . . The Society increased daily. . . . There it continued divers years.

It was hoped that a Library might be created and a charter of incorporation secured. The Library was to be entitled "the Library of Queen Elizabeth". The society was to become the "Academy for the Study of Antiquities and History founded by Queen Elizabeth". The queen was asked to make contributions "out of her gracious library" and it was hoped to secure "a convenient room in the Savoy or the late dissolved mónastery of St. John's of Jerusalem". It was urged in favour of the formation of such a body that there were important records "whereof the originals are extant in the hands of some private gentlemen".

This Society will not be hurtful to any of the Universities . . . for this Society tendeth to the preservation of history and antiquitie of which the universities, long busied in the arts take little care or regard.

A petition on behalf of this design was actually presented to the queen.

It is interesting to note the kind of people who constituted this antiquarian society—and especially the predominance of the legal profession within it. Spelman says that they met "every Friday weekly in the Term". Hearne states, "many of them [were] students in the inns of court", and on the refounding of the society in 1614 he tells us that the surviving members were joined by "several of the most eminent lawyers of that time". Heralds, genealogists and keepers of records were among the number, but the lawyers seem to have constituted the greater part of the society.

At this point we see the beginning of a more scientific mode of enquiry into the antiquities of England. Out of mere antiquarianism and the lawyers' hunt for precedents, a new kind of history was being born to supersede the old compilations from the chroniclers. It was a kind of history that went behind the chroniclers, and surpassed the old narrations by the analysis of institutions and laws; and it led to the discovery, the collection and the diligent study of manuscripts, many of which were gathered into the famous library of Sir Robert Cotton. In the Society of Antiquaries an attempt was made to discover how far back one could trace the High Court of Parliament or the office of Lord Chancellor, how ancient were Christianity and heraldry and towns in England. Tate, the secretary of the Society, wrote a paper on Star Chamber while Agard wrote on funeral ceremonies, sterling money, forest-laws, the history of lawful combat, the antiquities and privileges of the Inns of Court, and the terms defining the dimensions of land in England. Professor Hazeltine (writing in *Cambridge Legal Essays*, p. 168) helps us to understand this movement when he calls attention to the "Gothic revival"—a renaissance of medieval law and custom, in the 16th and 17th centuries. We must also remember that the thread upon which our whole story hangs is the persistence of the English common law and the strength of our legal traditions in the Tudor period.

The Defects in Historical Technique

It is important that we should understand the deficiencies of historical technique at the opening of the 17th century. We must remember that historical scholarship at its beginning naturally sees the past with the eyes of the present, without realizing the need for mental adjustments and transpositions. Sometimes the men whom we are studying were astonishingly credulous in their conception of the historical background at a given moment, astonishingly naïve

C

in their attitude to what we might call general history, wildly anachronistic in their picture of the condition of things in Anglo-Saxon times. Even at the Society of Antiquaries a man could throw out casually (as though it were still the accepted truth) the view that the ancient Britons were the descendants of the Trojans. These students did not possess the apparatus for the correct dating of documents; and all the combined faults of their historical method ensured that they should err in one direction—in the ante-dating of their sources, (as we have already seen in the case of the *Mirror of Justice*). Such mistakes were bound to be common at a time when men did not yet conceive of history as development, when on the contrary the Renaissance had taken over from classical writers a theory of decline. Historians had still to learn how the pattern of life and the structure of society change in successive epochs, so that each century has its peculiar quality. In any case the golden age was still in the past, and writers were able to say that the ancient laws were best, the older precedent was more valuable than the Tudor practice, and freedom had been perfect in Anglo-Saxon times. Liberty in fact did not have to be created or hatched or evolved or nursed into existence. It only needed to be restored.

The interests and activities of these men were antiquarian. They delighted in the hunt for precedents. They did not attempt to examine each precedent in its appropriate context—to see it in its contemporary setting and its proper bearings—but would fly away with it, transposing it directly into their Stuart age. In any case, the English common law—so strong in its appeal to the past, its insistence on continuity and its reverence for precedents—may have made the English lawyers fervent students of the middle ages, but did not give them the point of view of the modern historian. Coke more than once attacked the chroniclers for their misunderstanding of legal matters, and at a later date Sir Roger Twysden in his *Considerations* attempted to reply on behalf of the general historian. The limitations of the lawyers, particularly those which are relevant to our present argument, are perhaps best described in Maitland's essay, *Why the History of English Law is not written:*

A lawyer finds on his table a case about rights of common which sends him to the Statute of Merton. But is it really the law of 1236 that he wants to know? No, it is the ultimate result of the interpretations set on the statute by the judges of twenty generations. The more modern the decision the more valuable for his purpose. *That process by which old principles and old phrases are charged with a new content, is from the lawyer's point of view an evolution of the true intent and meaning of the old law; from the historian's point of view it is almost of necessity a process of perversion and misunderstanding* [my italics].

Sir Henry Spelman was wiser than many of the historical writers of the 17th century and in some respects he was more aware than most of his contemporaries of the differences between the past and the present. It was he whom Maitland described as having "had the chief part in introducing the feudal system into England"—a fact which at least enabled him to have a better vision of the past than Coke, who had no conception of feudal law. In the introduction to one of his works, *Of Parliaments*, he has a passage in which he seems to be guarding himself against some of the errors just described; he shows how "succeeding Ages viewing what is past by the present conceive the former to have been like to that they live in". Dealing with the parliaments of antiquity, he decides to regard them as out of the range of modern controversies—"like the siege of Troy, matters only of Story and Discourse". Writing *Of the Ancient Government of England*, he said:

To tell the Government of *England* under the old *Saxon* Laws, seemeth a *Utopia* to us present; strange and uncouth; yet can there be no period assign'd, wherein either the frame of those Laws was abolished or this of ours entertained; but as Day and Night creep insensibly, one upon the other, so also hath this Alteration grown upon us insensibly, every age altering something, and no age seeing more than what themselves are Actors in, nor thinking it to have been otherwise than as themselves discover it by the present.

This man clearly went much further than any of his contemporaries towards the understanding of the processes of history. It is not strange that it should have been Spelman rather than Coke who realized the past as something structurally different from the present. It is not strange that Spelman should have avoided many of the mistakes of the other historians of the time.

The Historians and the Stuarts

We are told that the meetings of the Society of Antiquaries were discontinued in 1604, partly because of the death of many of its chief supporters and partly because of "the jealousy of King James I suspecting their loyalty and attachment to his government". Spelman describes how, when an attempt was made to revive the Society in 1614, the rule was adopted "That for avoiding Offence, we should neither meddle with Matters of State nor of Religion".

But before our next Meeting we had notice that His Majesty took a little Mislike to our Society; not being inform'd that we had resolv'd to decline all Matters of State. Yet hereupon we forebore to meet again.

At one stage it was argued that the Society would be "prejudicial to certain great and learned bodies".

Nor were there wanting very powerful men that proved enemies to them, and among other things, they were pleased to alledge, that some of the society were persons not only disaffected to, but really of a quite different persuasion from, the Church of England.

There exists a copy of a summons to "Mr Stow" to a meeting of the Society in the 41st year of Elizabeth's reign. Among other things it says:

It is desired that you bringe none other with you, nor geue anie notice unto anie, but to such as have the like summons.

James I appears to have recognized the danger at an early stage. He was hostile to the Society of

Antiquaries and jealous of the historical materials collected in the library of Sir Robert Cotton. In 1621 he showed great anxiety to have the papers of Sir Edward Coke examined. The manuscripts of both Coke and Cotton were taken over by Charles I at a subsequent period. It was inevitable that, in the new kind of history that was being produced, the dice should be loaded against the king before the enquiry started. A concession once extracted in the past, a privilege once granted by a monarch, was a right and a precedent to be reasserted in the present, whatever might have happened during the intervening period. We shall see that a single, remote and dubious example might be used as the basis for the declaration of a permanent constitutional principle. We must not say that these men merely read their politics into their history. On the contrary it seems to have been rather their history that gave a new turn to their political views. Their history can be sufficiently accounted for as a result of their defective technique. And even Spelman, who has been described as "a devoted royalist", could not deny the historical interpretations that provoked the Petition of Right.

From the early 17th century, however, the antiquarians were moving against the monarchical positions, though Cotton still was consulted and used by the king and it was said of Selden that he had the confidence of both sides—he was approached by the Commons when they were attacking the royal prerogative and by the Lords when they were defending their rights. James I often discussed antiquarian topics with members of the group. From 1620, however, the historians are working passionately against the monarchical claims, Coke is producing his most damaging work, the debates in the House of Commons take a more historical turn, often seeming "rather to have resembled arguments in a court of law than debates in a legislative assembly"; and "the ancient records both of the courts and of the House were often produced and read"; till, on the eve of Charles I's third Parliament, the opposition leaders, Eliot, Wentworth and Pym, meet Selden and Coke at Cotton's house to formulate their House of Commons policy. At this stage of the proceedings there can be no doubt that political prejudice came in to add to the effect of the original aberrations.

If the age itself leaned to a certain interpretation and even a certain kind of error in its historical study —throwing too many of the ideas of the 17th century into its reconstruction of the middle ages—we can easily conceive that the errors were accentuated when the common reader appropriated the results of this scholarship. If men like Spelman, Cotton and Selden were able to escape some of the wilder exaggerations of the period, the less scholarly public found the new interpretations more irresistible, more self-evidently right than the historians themselves. The more extreme school—Sir Edward Coke in particular —captured the politicians and the members of parliament. The cautions that might have checked the fervour of the public were the less operative in that the important works of Cotton and Spelman did not appear in print during the lifetime of their authors. It would appear that Spelman chose not to publish the second volume of his *Glossary* for example—the volume in which certain crucial words like *Parliamentum* were discussed. Antiquarian controversies gained in piquancy because the political and the historical issues were so closely intertwined.

We shall see that the 17th century the influence of the common law, the defects in historical technique and the conflict with the Stuarts combined to give rise to a whig interpretation that superseded the Tudor teaching examined in an earlier chapter. We shall see also how the famous lawyer, Sir Edward Coke, became not indeed the most reliable but the most influential of the representatives of the new historiography, and carried the whig tendencies to the wildest extremes.

IV. THE NEW HISTORY IN ITS RELATIONS WITH CURRENT POLITICS

The Antiquity of the House of Commons

IN the early years of Elizabeth's reign it was believed that the House of Commons went back to the time of Henry I. Even later, Stow in 1592 and Ralegh in 1615 referred the origin of Parliament to that period. In 1571, however, the 14th-century document, the *Modus Tenendi Parliamentum*, was published, and was held to be a description of the order of Parliament in the time of Edward the Confessor. Henceforward it came to be the general view that the House of Commons had been established long before the Norman Conquest, and even from time immemorial. Coke, for example, traced the House through Anglo-Saxon and Roman times and even found it amongst the ancient Britons. Some admitted that there was a break in the story after the Norman Conquest, and amongst these Henry I appeared in a new guise —as the restorer of Parliament. Towards the end of its period of life the Society of Antiquaries held a symposium on this subject, and some of the papers that have been published put forward the views described above.

It was possible to refer to "Parliaments composed of three degrees" in Roman times—namely "Senatores, equites and plebes". It was customary to quote "I, Ina, King of the West Saxons, have called all my fatherhood, aldermen and my wisest Commons". Canute, we are told, "held a parliament, though not then as stiled, but yet truly so to be accompted; and since it hath all the parts of our parliament we might rightly call it so. . . ." Edward the Confessor signed a charter at a Parliament *coram . . . omnibus optimatibus Angliae omnique populo audiente et vidente.* In the absence of evidence for the attendance of commoners, the historians were able to resort to certain subterfuges. Some writers said that the term *baro* included burgesses, that the citizens of London and the burgesses of the Cinque Ports were called barons. "There is an express authority that proveth that the word magnates comprehendeth the people." Others held the view that till the reign of Henry III all freemen could attend Parliament in person, but that after that date the privilege was contracted to a mere right to elect representatives.[1]

One writer at an early date resisted this tendency in historical interpretation. He was Arthur Hall, who

---

[1] Some time before 1592, Lambarde wrote in his *Archion*:

"In every quarter of the Realme a great many of *Burroughes* doe yet send *Burghesses* to the Parliament, which is nevertheless so ancient and so long decayed, and gon to nought, that it cannot be shewed that they have been of any reputation, at any time since the *Conquest*, and much lesse that they have obtained the priviledge by the grant of any King succeeding the same. . . .

"If they of ancient *Demeasnes*, have ever since the *Conquest*, prescribed not to send *burgesses* to the *parliament* then no doubt there was a *parliament* before the *Conquest* to the which *they of other places* did send these *burghesses*."

in his *Letter to F. A.* (1576) provided an early and breezy example of what the Americans would call "de-bunking". His adventure was to result in his imprisonment at the order of the House of Commons in 1581, because (as Bacon disclosed in a parliamentary speech in 1601)

he said the Lower House was a new person in the Trinity, and because these words tended to the derogation of the state of the house, and giving absolute power to the other.

The Britons, Hall conjectured, governed without our form of Parliament, "for I cannot perceive there was any state of nobility". The Romans merely "made conquest of the region, and annexed it to the Romayne auctority". The Anglo-Saxons had so many wars that they can have had no time for parliamentary government.[1] About Canute he is sarcastic: "Canutus the Dane . . . was absolute King of the whole Realme . . . his laws you have: see what you find there. So great conquerors do not commonly grant such large freedomes to subjects." He glances at the despotic character of the Danish monarchy in his own time and in all previous history, and wonders

[1] "And loke howe many kingdoms they erected, how long in warres before, how they continued, how they were brought to one Monarchie, and the sequele then, and you shall finde there was no leysure for Parliaments. . . . The Saxons kept themselves Kings here, though with much ado and great continual slaughters, not only with the ancient inhabitants of this land, but with themselves one king with another . . . but how far from the way of our Parliament your own discretion will conceive, if you have good consideration of the times, people and maner of lawing."

why Canute should have established a different form of government in a country that had been conquered.

He was not constrained at any time againste his will: for the poore Englishe nation, God knowes, were laide low enough. . . . Yet would I fain learn whether by Parliament and general consent of the three estates thereof, the excessive Tributs were graunted and the exaction called the *Dane gelt*. . . .

Hall, in fact, turns the tables on the supporters of the theory of an early House of Commons.

Till the twentith yere of Henrie the thirde I heare of no Parliament, unlesse you will have all consultations Parliaments. . . . I cannot meete with the name of the Knight of a Shire or Burges of Parliament, or any such men, mentioned tyl now of late dayes. . . .

And even after there is a Parliament, the authority still lies with the king, says Hall; and when legislation is effected it carries the formula "the King willeth or he commandeth. . . ." In the reigns of Henry III and Edward I Hall discovers accumulated instances: "Our soveraigne Lorde the King hath ordained . . . the King and his counsel have ordained. . . . We have also ordeined by the advise of our Councell at a Parliament . . . holden . . .", etc. etc.

Hall had a grudge against the House of Commons, as a result of a private dispute which had led to proceedings in Parliament. Before the House met again he was compelled to appear at the Privy Council, and in 1581, when the House was assembled, he was accused of publishing the debates and impugning the authority of the Commons. It was

unanimously resolved that he should be imprisoned
for six months or until he retracted, and further
should be fined 500 marks and excluded from the
House during the sitting of that Parliament. According to the Clerk of the House, the Commons were
especially indignant in that he had written "a false
and sclaunderous discourse against the Antiquitie
and Authoritie of the comon house". In his sub-
mission he said: "I . . . doe allowe of the ancient
authoritie of the common howse, wherein the third
estate of the whole Realme is duelie represented".

The whole controversy concerning the origin of
the House of Commons was to blaze out afresh in
the last quarter of the seventeenth century. The
whigs then showed their indignation even in the
House itself, because the view was put forward that
knights and burgesses were not summoned to Parliament till the reign of Henry III. Yet even earlier in
the century some distinguished antiquarians confessed that they could find no clear evidence before
the reign of Henry III—though it does not appear
that they published their views at this time. Spelman
did not believe that the House of Commons went
back to the time of Henry I, but when the second
part of his *Glossary* (the one which contained the
word *Parliamentum*) appeared after the Restoration,
its editors were charged with having tampered with
the text. Sir Robert Cotton avoided the more
flagrant errors of the early 17th-century historians
and was in close relations with James I till 1621.
In that year he wrote (but did not publish) an essay

entitled *That the Kings of England have been pleased usually to consult with their Peeres in the great Councell, and Commons in Parliament, of Marriage, Peace and Warre*. He describes how, after the Anglo-Norman period, the aristocracy "was like in time to strangle the Monarchie".

Though others foresaw the mischief betimes, yet none attempted the remedy, untill King *Iohn*, whose over-hasty undertakings, brought in those broyls of the Barons' Wars.

In *A briefe Discourse concerning the Power of the Peeres and Commons of Parliament in point of Judicature* Cotton continued the theme:

The deare experience *Henry* III himself had made at the Parliament at *Oxford* in the 40. yeare of his Raigne, and the memory of the many streights his Father was driven unto, especially at *Runn-mead* near *Stanes*, brought this K. wisely to begin what his Successors fortunately finished, in lessning the strength and power of his great Lords. And this was wrought by . . . weakning that hand of power which they carried in the Parliaments, by commanding the service of many Knights, Citizens and Burgesses to that great Councell. . . .

Perhaps because he was writing for the king, perhaps because at an earlier date he was more royalist in his sympathies, Cotton was more unfriendly to the Commons in *A Short View of the Long Reign of Henry III*, an essay, presented to James I:

The Commons, to whom days present seem ever worst, commend the foregone ages they never remembered and condemn the present though they know neither the disease nor the remedy.

There were some exceptions, then; but the prevailing view (and in particular the published writings) in the early 17th century ascribed great antiquity to the House of Commons. Nothing can have been more fitted to increase the self-confidence of that House in the time of James I than its conviction that it had existed from time immemorial—that, far from being a late and derivative body, it was an original and independent element in the government, coeval with the monarchy itself. The statements of the anti-royalist party contain frequent references to the antiquity of the House. And nothing can have served better than this assumption to convince men that the privileges of Parliament were not of royal grace but of inherent right.

The New History and the Common Law: Sir Edward Coke

The name of Sir Edward Coke, who lived from 1551 to 1634, is important in the development of English historical study, the evolution of the common law, and the parliamentary conflict with the early Stuarts. Coke used the historical methods of the time in order to magnify the claims of the common law; in order to codify our legal traditions in opposition to royal authority; and, particularly in the 1620's, in order to provide the House of Commons with material for a conflict with the crown on questions of historical interpretation. He helped to secure that the traditional system of English law should win the victory in the 17th century not only over the king but also over rival systems of law which could claim to be perhaps more efficient, perhaps even more up-to-date.

He could hardly have secured his objects without altering the character of the law; and this he achieved by a return to the past. He applied historical interpretation to the study of the common law—always using history with a purpose, however, always the advocate, using precedents (as a lawyer would) in order to make out a case. And, though he was very learned in legal precedents, it matters very much from our point of view that he was extremely credulous in regard to general history—the general story of pre-conquest England for example. He went to history for a polemical purpose, and between the time when he was a royal official (Queen Elizabeth's attorney-general) and the time when he was in opposition, fighting the Stuart conception of monarchy, his legal views on some matters relating to the royal prerogative underwent a change. When the crown lawyers attacked his historical interpretations, they were more in conformity with the legal tradition that had been handed down to them than he was. In some ways they were also closer to the interpretation which would be given by historians of the present day. While he was alive, the reaction against some of his historical teaching was already beginning and from the middle of the century, and especially after the Restoration, it gathered weight. The whole succeeding development of historical study, down almost to the present day, has been a withdrawal from the position which he took up. His activity had a great effect on the development of historical study as well as the evolution of the common law. His was the work that was popularized, that the Long Parliament ordered to be published, that influenced the pamphleteers. He is almost the extreme example of the whig interpretation of history. When his end was approaching, in 1631, Charles I ordered that on his death his papers should be secured, "for he is held too great an oracle among the people, and they may be misled by anything that carries such an authority as all things do which he either speaks or writes".

It was fitting that he should be a great worshipper of the past. He thought that the older the law was, the more lofty and pure it must be estimated. It has been said that he was almost prepared to justify trial by battle as something more than an anachronism, out of his worship of the ancient ways. He regretted that some of the complicated legal procedure of the middle ages had gone out of use. If he had secured all that he wished it would seem that England would have been locked and imprisoned in the systematization that he had produced of our medieval law. In his Seventh Report he writes:

Interroge pristinam generationem (for out of the old fields must come the new corn) and diligently search out the judgements of our forefathers: and that for divers reasons. First on our owne fact . . . we are but of yesterday (and therefore had need of the wisdom of those that were before us) and had

been ignorant (if we had not received light and knowledge from our forefathers) and our daies upon the
earth are but as a shadow in respect of the old and
auncient daies and times past, wherein the lawes
have been by the wisdom of the most excellent men,
in many successions of ages, by long and continuall
experience (the triall of right and truth) fined and
refined, which no one man (being of so short a time)
albeit hee had in his head the wisdome of all the
men in the world, in any one age could never have
effected or attained unto. . . . No man ought to take
upon him to be wiser than the laws.

Again he says "That old Laws and new Meats are
fittest for use". Also: "It hath long been an old
Rule in Policy that Correctio legum est evitanda".

Next, he believed in the antiquity of the laws of
England—believed indeed that the common law,
the common-law courts and the House of Commons
itself went back to the age before the Norman Conquest, even to time immemorial. He writes in one
place:

The Lawes of England are of much more antiquity,
then they are reported to be, and more then any of
the constitutions or lawes Imperiall of the Romaine
Emperours.

London, he said, was founded before the time of
Romulus and Remus, and still retained the laws of
that early date. Trial by jury, in his opinion, existed
before the Norman Conquest. He had no conception
of feudal law, and because of this, says Maitland, "he
was utterly unable to give any connected account of
the law that he knew so well".

When he was Speaker of the House of Commons in 1592–1593 he made before the queen a "most elaborate Speech on the Dignity and Antiquity of Parliaments". Elsewhere he tells us that no doubt at one time both houses sat together. He also put forward the view that the Commons were a judicial court, because they had the power to adjourn themselves. He tells us:

It is the law and Custom of the Parliament when any new device is moved on the King's behalf in Parliament, for aydes and the like, to answer that in this new device, they dare not agree without Conference with their Counties; whereby it appeareth that such conference is warrantable by the law and custom of Parliament.

Further, he wrote:

That the Laws of the Antient Britains, their Contracts and other Instruments, and the Records and Judicial proceedings of their Judges were Written and Sentenced in the Greek Tongue, it is plain and evidenced by proofs, luculent and uncontroulable.

His philology was equally curious. Parliament came from "parler la ment", he said. "In French *coins* signifieth a corner, because in ancient times money was square with corners." [1]

---

[1] He was deceived by the *Modus Tenendi Parliamentum* (which Selden, however, said was later than the time of Edward II). Prynne, one of his later critics, asserts: "Not one of all our ancient Historians . . . I have perused ever made the least mention of it before Sir Edward Cooke vouched it in the Parliament of 35 Eliz. An. 1592, when he was Speaker". Similarly Coke was deceived in regard to the date of the *Mirror of Justice* and other documents.

We have seen that, according to Maitland, a lawyer is less concerned to discover what the Statute of Merton meant to the 13th century than to learn what has been the final result of the interpretations that have been put upon it since. Coke the lawyer, however, has to be at tension with Coke the student of antiquities, and it is not always easy to say where the decision will lie between the two. It is true that, in accordance with Maitland's thesis, he can assert that his interpretations of ancient law are based on the judgments of the courts. On these occasions he is behaving as a lawyer would, and his judgments are liable therefore to be "unhistorical". Yet he could speak rather as an historian and assert: "Ancient Charters, whether they be before time of memory or after, ought to be construed as the Law was taken when the Charter was made and according to ancient allowance". As we shall see, he was in fact able to interpret *Magna Carta* not according to the practice of the courts up to his time, and not by reference to the age of John, but by the use of 14th-century instances—that is to say, by reference to the most favourable period between the two.

Sliding thus between the lawyer's and the historian's mode of reasoning, he could fasten England more tightly than before under a system of law that was medieval; while yet by a method which the historian would regard as leading to anachronism, he could turn this medieval law into something that in reality was in many ways unlike the middle ages. In fact he did something new with the history. The common law could never have imposed itself on the times if there had not been the confusions of thought or the elasticities of interpretation that enabled Coke to turn it into something more like the 17th century. And, as Maitland has said, for the lawyer in future our "medieval common law" was to be not anything absolutely medieval at all, but simply the common law of a later age of interpretation, and particularly of Coke. "Out of the old fields must the new corn come", said Coke himself. For all his glorification of antiquity he showed little trace of conservatism in his judgments, we are told by Plucknett. He would quote "passably good Latin maxims with an air of antiquity"—and yet it turns out that sometimes he had simply invented these himself.

It is not clear that the common law, as it had come down from the time of the Tudors, would have been an unsurmountable obstruction to the despotic exercise of the royal power in the age of the Stuarts. Coke's teaching made the difference, though it was ineffective so long as judges in the courts gave their verdicts in favour of the prerogative. This renders all the more important the alliance Coke made with the parliamentary opposition and the leadership he acquired in the House of Commons especially after 1620. It is impossible, however, to close one's eyes to a factor which conditioned even his historical interpretations. This was his sheer professional jealousy, the aggrandizing spirit of a practitioner of the common law.

We must remind ourselves that the weaknesses Coke might have had as a general historian did not prevent his being one of the greatest of English lawyers. If he gave a new turn to the law by what purported to be an appeal to the past, this was itself the mark of a creative mind that was able to achieve practical results by virtue of an added technical ability. He more than anybody else translated medieval limitations upon the monarchy into 17th-century terms; and if he transposed feudal safeguards into common-law restrictions, still his anachronistic sins became a service to the cause of liberty. All that he did helped to confirm the view that in England the king is under the law, and conspired to bring that view of English government to a more complete and vivid realization. This at least was a genuine legacy of the middle ages, and one which perhaps the Tudor monarchy and the early Stuart pretensions were tending to destroy. Though it were by tricks and elisions, Coke secured the retention of an attitude to monarchy which became part of the continuity of our history. And even those who might deplore the Civil War would hardly wish to unwind the history that bears the mark of his influence.

Nullus liber homo

There is little sign of the importance of *Magna Carta* until the Parliament of 1610, and the document had hardly saved Englishmen from the dangers of despotism in the time of the Tudors. Since this was the case we must not imagine that the Charter itself was for all time an all-sufficient guarantee for our liberties, or that it ratified and sealed them for ever. The history of England after the Tudors turned *Magna Carta* once again into the effective cornerstone of our liberties; but the discovery of its importance, the revival of the popular memory of it, comes late, comes like an after-thought, and attains great significance in the 17th century. The Tudor age would never have relished the idea that the king should be limited by feudal law—they remembered too well the over-mighty subject, the danger of private rights that menaced the state. The glory of the Tudor age lay in the opposite movement in fact —the victory that the monarch had achieved over feudal limitations and over the whole realm of privilege.

Coke, however, interpreted *Magna Carta* as an affirmation not of feudal law but of the common law. By a subtle elision he aggrandized the common law and demonstrated more plainly its superiority over the monarch himself. He and the opposition lawyers secured the resurrection of the document, not reaching a historical comprehension of it, but attacking the legal interpretations which had been current down to their time. They envisaged it in terms which the 17th century could understand. Thus the Charter once again became a landmark in our history, because thinking made it so.

Coke's commentary would appear to have been written by 1628 and is the first notable disquisition on the Charter. It formed part of the second volume of the *Institutes* which opened with volume one in the above-mentioned year. In 1640 one of Coke's sons moved in the House of Commons that Sir Edward's papers (impounded by the king after his death) should be delivered to Sir Robert his heir; and on the 12 May 1641 Sir Robert was ordered "to publish in print the commentary on Magna Carta, the Pleas of the Crowne and the jurisdiction of courts, according to the intention of the said Sir Edward Coke". Apart from Blackstone and a work of no great importance to our purpose in the 19th century, this was the only genuine commentary on the subject until very recent times—indeed until the "myth of *Magna Carta*" was (perhaps too completely) exploded for students of the 20th century.

The revival of *Magna Carta* grew out of an interest in one particular clause, the famous *Nullus liber homo* clause, which gives a guarantee against arbitrary imprisonment. It was early discovered that English legal traditions, contemporary judicial practice and parliamentary statutes actually contravened the apparent sense of this chapter. The anomaly itself created some agitation and had been pointed out in the *Mirror of Justice* which from 1550 was being read in manuscript. Francis Tate, in a paper on *Camera Stellata* read to the Society of Antiquaries, tried to account for the discrepancy; and showed how, in order to secure justice, the king had been compelled "to resort to his absolute power again". Ralegh in his *Prerogative of Parliament* raised the question of the imprisonment of the subject by the crown for "reasons of state", and suggested that a case of this kind would lead to a demand for the confirmation of the Charter in Parliament. He was prophetic, for not only were there attempts in the Commons to settle the interpretation of the *Nullus liber homo* clause, but the Petition of Right arose out of a parliamentary debate on this chapter of the Charter, after Charles I had imprisoned the Five Knights. Finally, Coke's richest comments on the Charter are contained in his discussion of this chapter; and it was clearly his interpretation, (admittedly a novel interpretation even for him, and actually inconsistent with decisions he had given on the bench and speeches he had made in the House of Commons,) which led to the Petition of Right. The debate on the *Nullus liber homo* clause, which issued in the Petition of Right, is the great historic moment for Coke personally and for the new historiography, as we shall see. It brings to a climax the intervention of the historian (as such) in practical politics at this time.

The following was then Chapter 29 of the Charter of 9 Henry III and on this chapter Coke makes some of his most interesting comments:

No free man shall be arrested, or detained in prison, or deprived of his freehold, or his liberties or free customy or outlawed or exiled, or in any other way molested; and we will not set forth against him nor send against him, unless by the lawful judgment of his peers and by the law of the land. . . .

It was the view of Coke that the Charter only

reaffirmed more ancient constitutional rights; that statutes contrary to its provisions were void; and that legal judgments which contravened it were invalid. On Chapter 29 he writes:

This extends to Villeins, saving against their Lord, for they are free against all men, saving against their lord. . . .

Upon this Chapter, as out of a roote, many fruit-full branches of the law of England have sprung. And therefore first the genuine sense hereof is to be seen and after how the same hath been declared, and interpreted. . . .

That no man be taken or imprisoned but *per legem terrae*, that is, by Common Law, Statute Law or Custome of *England*. . . . No man shall be disseised . . . unless it be by the lawfull judgement, that is, verdict of his equals, (that is men of his own con-dition) or by the Law of the Land (that is to speak it once for all) by the due course, and processe of Law.

Coke attacks, as an infringement of this "funda-mental law", an act of Henry VII's reign "by colour of which" horrible oppressions were committed by the notorious Empson and Dudley.

The word *libertates* in this chapter of the Charter gives him the opportunity to enlarge on the liberties of Englishmen. Speaking of these he says that in the first place they are simply the Laws of the Realm such as are comprised in the present Charter. In the second place they are:

the freedomes that the Subjects of England have: For example the Company of the *Merchant Taylors* of England, having power by their Charter to make

Ordinances, made an Ordinance that every brother of the same Society should put the one half of his clothes to be dressed by some Clothworker free of the same Company upon pain to forfit x⁵ . . . and it was adjudged that this Ordinance was against the Law, because it was against the Liberty of the Subject, for every subject hath freedome to put his clothes to be dressed by whom he wil. . . . And so it is if such or the like grant had been made by his Letters Patents.

Thirdly, *libertates* are the "franchises and privileges which the Subjects have of the gift of the King or which the subjects claim by prescription".

If a grant be made to any man, to have the sole making of Cards or the sole dealing with any other trade, that grant is against the liberty, and freedome of the Subject . . . and consequently against this great Charter.

Generally, then, all monopolies are against Chapter 29 of the Charter, because they deprive a free man of his liberty.

Coke's views on the general interpretation of Chapter 29 of the Charter—and on the meaning of *Lex terrae* in particular—were highly controversial and had changed in comparatively recent times. The issue was important—it concerned the crown's right to imprison subjects for reasons of state, and the question of continuing such detention after the crown had refused to divulge the reason for it. The discrepancy gave Coke's opponents a considerable tactical advantage in the debates to which his interpretation gave rise, preparatory to the drawing-up of the Petition of Right. During the debates he produced a precedent from the reign of Edward III, to show that a committal without the naming of the reason had been deemed insufficient by the judges. He supported his view by quoting the words spoken by Festus to King Agrippa in the last verse of the twenty-fifth chapter of the Acts of the Apostles:

For it seemeth to me unreasonable to send a prisoner, and not withal to signify the crimes *laid* against him.

On behalf of the crown a former Resolution of the King's Bench, dated 1615, was produced four days later, on 29 March. It then transpired that Coke himself had signed the Resolution, which approved the doctrine that the cause of imprisonment need not be disclosed. Gardiner writes:

Even Coke was for once disconcerted. The report, he said, was not yet twenty-one years old. Then floundering still more deeply in the mire and forgetting dates and everything else in his confusion, he began telling wildly of the necessity of dealing strictly at that time with the traitors concerned in the Gunpowder Plot, as if, in 1615, every one of them who had fallen into the hands of the government had not been executed nine years before. . . . Two days later Coke was himself again. He had the right, he said, of changing his opinion when his knowledge was increased. Since he signed the resolution referred to he had seen members of Parliament imprisoned. He had himself only just escaped imprisonment.

Over a fortnight later the attack was pushed further, when the Attorney-General referred to the opinion of the judges in 13 James I, in Runell's case. He quoted:

Coke, Crooke, Dodderidge, and Haughton, justices, did hold, that a return that one is committed per mandatum private consilii domini regis, was good enough, without returning any cause; for it is not fit that the arcana imperii should be disclosed.

Coke replied that he did not pretend to have "veritatem ex cathedra or infallibility of spirit". The Attorney-General made another interesting contribution to the history of Coke's earlier views on the subject of *Magna Carta*, and particularly on the question which was so important in connexion with the Petition of Right—the question whether a man committed to prison by the king or his council had the right to bail. He showed how in 1621 Coke on two separate occasions had addressed the House to the effect that *Magna Carta* had no application to this particular case. Coke, in fact, had induced the House to abandon the project of an Act of Parliament to interpret Chapter 29 of the Charter, an Act which would have required bail to be granted to men who had been imprisoned for reasons of state. Coke's attitude was to be very different when the project was renewed at the time of the Petition of Right.

His attitude is already different in the *Institutes*, as we have seen; and here he adds, on the *Nullus liber homo* clause:

But since we wrote these things . . . see now the Petition of Right 3 Charles 1 . . . which hath made an end of this question if any were.

As the gold-finer will not out of the dust threds or shreds of gold let passe the least crum in respect of the excellency of the mettal. so ought not the learned Reader to let passe any syllable of this Law in respect of the excellency of the matter.

The Victory of the New History

We have reached the point at which the House of Commons definitely moves over to the whig interpretation of history. In a classic conflict the fruits of the antiquarian researches are thrown into the arena, and, by contemporary admission, the results reverberate. At one of the great moments in 17th-century parliamentary history, the debate turns on the construction of a clause in *Magna Carta*; and those who merely represent the continuation of Tudor legal practice are confronted by men who have discovered fresh material in the middle ages, men who, returning to old fields, have found new corn, and are eager to tell the world of their discovery.

In the 1620's the work of the historians had evidently been developing to a climax. The imprisonment of certain men who had refused to contribute to the loan of 1626 provided them with their opportunity. When five of the knights concerned appealed to the King's Bench for *Habeas Corpus*, Selden was one of the counsel employed on their behalf. There does not seem to have been on anybody's part a denial that *Magna Carta* was still valid, but the judges refused to accept an interpretation of it drawn from certain statutes of Edward III, which they said did not apply to cases of committal by the king. At the same time the judges carefully abstained from a decision in favour of the claim that the crown could go on committing without ever showing cause. The men who had refused to contribute to the loan were released just over a month later (2 January 1628), and on the 30 January the king ordered the issue of writs for a new Parliament. It has been said that it was proposed for a moment to publish a proclamation excluding all lawyers from the Parliament. On 17 March 1628, a few days before the opening of the proceedings, the leading members of the Commons talked with the historians at Sir Robert Cotton's house on Palace Yard. Soon afterwards the controversy had taken the course which issued in the drawing-up of the Petition of Right. It is notable that in this period, when *Magna Carta* was being brought to public attention, two copies of the original are said to have found their way into the hands of Sir Robert Cotton.

Almost from the opening of the discussions on the imprisonment of the Five Knights we learn the importance of the contribution that the historians had to make. The debate was not limited to *Magna Carta* and produced the resurrection of many ancient statutes that guaranteed the liberties of Englishmen. On the 25 March a certain Mr. Creskeld (who must have learned of the matter by report, since he was not present on that occasion) referred to an impressive historical exposition which Coke had recently given on the subject of the Statute of Westminster. At the opening conference that took place between Lords and Commons on the question of the detention of the Five Knights, an imposing tribute was made to the recent achievements in scholarship. The following is the report of the occasion:

Sir Dudley Diggs hoped to begin the conference, auspiciously, with an observation out of Holy Writ. In the days of good King Josiah, when the land was purged of idolatry and the great men went about to repair the house of God; whilst money was sought for, there was found a Book of the Law, which had been neglected. He was confident, that we would as cheerfully, join with them, in acknowledging God's Blessings in our good King Josiah, as they did . . . so now, while they were seeking for money, they found, he could not say a book of our law, but main and fundamental points of the law neglected and broken; and this occasioned their desire of a conference. Wherein he was commanded to shew, That the laws of England are grounded on reason, more ancient than books, consisting much in unwritten customs, yet so full of justice and true equity, that your most honourable . . . ancestors often defended them with a nolumus mutari; and so ancient, that, from the Saxon days, notwithstanding the injuries and ruins of time, they have continued in most part the same.

Sir Benjamin Rudyard, who was anxious not to bring matters to extremities, spoke at a later date as though it were victory enough to have had *Magna Carta* brought out into the world again.

For my own part, I shall be very glad to see that good, old decrepid law of Magna Charta, which hath been so long kept in and lain bed-rid as it were; I should be glad, I say, to see it walk abroad again, with new vigour and lustre, attended by the other six statutes. For, questionless, it will be a general heartening to all.

Mr. Hakewell was in favour of moderation, and was ready to be satisfied with only a confirmation of the existing laws. He, too, paid tribute to what had been achieved by those historico-legal researches which had brought ancient statutes back into the public mind.[1]

In the ensuing discussions the king made it known that he held himself bound by *Magna Carta*, but that "the interpretation is left to the judges and to his great Council, and all is to be regulated by the common law". The king was induced to state that he would never again imprison men merely for refusing to contribute to a loan. The opposition lawyers for their part confessed that in time of danger a king might be compelled to imprison people without showing cause—rather in the way the Habeas

---

[1] "Although we have no more than a confirmation of those laws . . . we shall depart hence in far better case than when we came; and that in divers respects. 1st, Some of the laws recited in this bill, and desired to be confirmed, are not printed laws; they are known to few professors of the law, and much less to others; and yet they are laws of as great consequence to the Liberty of the Subject, if not of greater, than any that are printed . . . 2ndly will not the occasion of the making of this law of confirmation so notoriously known, be transmitted to all posterity? Certainly it will never be forgotten."

D

Corpus Act has to be suspended sometimes. In answer to the charge that a declaration of the cause of imprisonment might betray secrets of state or defeat the ends of justice, the opposition answered that they did not insist upon a particular cause, and that a general cause, such as treason, suspicion of treason, or felony would serve their purposes. The Attorney-General answered that in this case the current formula, *per mandatum domini regis*, would be equally to the point: though it was argued for the Commons that judges "by the intention of the law" were of the king's council and might safely be entrusted with secrets of state.

The real issue, however, was the interpretation of *Magna Carta*, and the problem of *per legem terrae* became the absorbing topic in the highest court in the land. Littleton, one of the opposition speakers, declared that "This was a great cause and peradventure the greatest that ever was in Christendom". The meaning of the *Nullus liber homo* clause had apparently formed the subject of a bill in the Commons in the reign of Elizabeth. Another bill had been put forward in 1621, but Coke himself had helped to prevent any enactment at that period. In the debates of the year 1628 the Bishop of Norwich "mervaylls that as yett since Magna charta we know not what is lex terre"; the Bishop of Lincoln "conceives that by Lex terrae is meant the Lawe of Edward the Confessor". Another speaker tells us "that the custome of England, tyme out of mynde is the law of England". The supporters of the king

argued that "the law of the land" included ecclesiastical laws, admiralty jurisdiction, martial law, the
law merchant, etc., and not merely the common law.
The Attorney-General says "how far lex terrae extends, is, and ever was the question". On another
occasion he repeats his thesis: "But how this lex
terrae is to be expounded, is the main apple of
contention".

The judges had been delivering their opinion in
the common-law courts for a long time. We have
already had a glimpse of the verdicts of Sir Edward
Coke during the reigns of Elizabeth and James I.
The Attorney-General during a conference between
Lords and Commons in 1628 said:

I appeal to you all, whether, if this should be held
for a direction, I may not truly say 'In hoc erravimus
omnes'? . . . What hath been the use and practice
in all ages, in these cases, appears by many precedents.

The Lord Chief Justice said: "If we have erred,
erravimus cum fratribus". He added: "I know not
any statute that goeth so far as that the king may
not commit". According to one report, Mr. Justice
Doddridge, who was concerned in the Five Knights
case, said, "Seeke them tymes of King John when
yt [i.e. the Charter] was made"—meaning, presum-
ably, that if you go back to history, you must go
back to the reign of John. Another judge made
the declaration, "These are only new inventions to
trouble old records". Perhaps there was point also
in Dodderidge's thesis: "A precedent that hath run

in a storm doth not much direct us in point of law; and records are the best testimonies".

The king finally made it known that he would agree to a bill to confirm *Magna Carta*:

but so as it may be without additions, paraphrases or explanations. . . . If ye seek to tye your King by new, and indeed impossible, bonds, you must be accountable to God and the country for the ill success of this meeting.

Charles admitted that the liberties of Englishmen were "not of grace but of right", and the Lord Keeper, speaking on his behalf, quoted James I's words: "He is no King, but a tyrant, that governs not by law". Charles, however, "would not have his prerogative straitened by any new explanation of *Magna Carta*". The Lords desired to humour the king in this matter—they were prepared to insist on the Charter itself but not to impose an interpretation of it by statute. Coke discovered a way out of the difficulty. He said: "Let us put up a Petition of Right." To the Lords he said that the Petition was drawn up "according to antient precedents"; but the technique employed—the Petition that was made to look like a statute—had aspects that were novel; the antiquarian elements in the case were mixed into new combinations: out of the old fields new corn was coming. On a later occasion Coke said "that this Petition . . . contained . . . a true exposition of the Great Charter". Its object was to impose the new interpretation of Chapter 29 in a manner that would be binding on the King and the courts.

The New Shape of English History

THE theory of primitive Teutonic freedom—a theory so exalted by Lilburne that he regarded the whole period since the Norman Conquest as a fall from grace; the "myth of *Magna Carta*", as Coke interpreted it in his treatises and in debate; the antiquity and independence of the House of Commons, as this came to be regarded in the latter part of Elizabeth's reign; and finally the idealization of the "constitutional experiments" of the 14th and 15th centuries—the attempt to continue English history in fact from this basis as though the Tudors had never intervened—these present us with the scaffolding of the whig interpretation. These are the things which, taken together, give the backbone of the whig structure of English history.

But we must not forget what is the whig interpretation of history *par excellence*—the interpretation of the constitutional conflict of the 17th century itself. And in this connexion we must note that the older writers confront us with an inversion of the particular structure which we to-day would perhaps expect that interpretation to have. They do not give us an organization of English history for the purpose of expounding the growth of freedom, the evolution of the constitution, the widening of those rights of

Englishmen that grow from precedent to precedent. At least if they do this, it is only one aspect of their work. Their history is based on the assumption that English liberty existed from the earliest times. The Norman Conquest may produce an aberration—a period of usurpation and tyranny—but even so, the ancient liberties are never quite forgotten. The Stuart monarchs stand condemned before the battle begins—they are undermining a constitution established in immemorial antiquity. Even in the light of post-Conquest history the Stuarts are regarded as the innovators and aggressors. They are attacking a known tradition; they are breaking established rules of the constitution; they are the enemies of the historic rights of Englishmen.

We at the present day might imagine that the British "constitution" at the beginning of the 17th century was still in the melting-pot—awaiting almost a hundred years of conflict that was to decide the seat of sovereignty and the division of power. To us the meaning of ancient precedents, (as that meaning stood in the year 1600,) might be doubtful—clouded by cases that pointed both ways, some of them against the king, and some of them (perhaps even the more recent ones) in favour of the prerogative. In some respects, we might say, the Puritans and Parliamentarians were even the innovators, seeking to exploit the financial difficulties of the crown in order to procure for the House of Commons greater power than it had had before.

For Coke and his friends, however, the British

constitution was older than the Charter, older than the Norman Conquest, and the Stuart kings were twisting the very history of England into a new channel. For them the meaning of ancient precedents was not doubtful; those which seemed to point the wrong way were no precedents at all; like the Norman Conquest they were mere anomalies and abuses·of power. The whig interpretation, when applied to the 17th century itself, is nothing but this attitude. It, too, is the work of Coke and his contemporaries therefore.

The whig interpretation began as a step in the direction of a deeper understanding of English history. The whig historians have not been harmful in what their sympathies enabled them to discern; they have only been harmful at those points where there is an arrest or suspension of sympathy. When Coke used the interpretations of Edward III's reign in support of his exposition of *Magna Carta*, he was perhaps a curious lawyer in that he went so far back, and a curious historian in that he did not go further back to the reign of John, but he was moving towards a historical point of view. Professor Powicke in the *Magna Carta Commemoration Essays* (1917, p. 97) has shown how 14th-century interpretations can be used to support a whiggish exposition of this document. Something like a whig interpretation in fact had begun to develop at a certain period in the middle ages; and in any case Coke was working for the continuity of English history, binding the middle ages and modern times more closely together. There can be no doubt that he used to good purpose the opportunities afforded by the common law and historical learning in order to impose upon the whole English story a directing idea.

It was a good thing to haul the country back to full consciousness of a conception that had a genuine meaning in medieval times—the doctrine that the king was under the law. And though James I and Charles I did not deny this fact in the way that some have imagined, it was good that in working out its implications we should have gone back to our medieval history, instead of taking our bearings (as we otherwise were naturally doing) from the more recent Tudor reigns. The common law and the whig interpretation have worked together to tighten the bonds that hold the Englishman to his past—have helped to foster our love of precedent, our affection for tradition, our desire for gradualness in change, our adherence to ancient liberties. The whig interpretation itself may be transformed without being overthrown—it may concede a point here, make a strategical retreat there, re-state its case somewhere else, and seem to abandon all its original strongholds. Yet it is capable of being elasticity itself. Our English history is in fact a whig interpretation that has been wonderfully qualified and copiously overlaid.

The Reaction against the extreme Whig Interpretation

The development of historical study in this country since the time of Coke has been the gradual toning-down of this initial whig interpretation, the curbing of the extravagances associated with its first exuberant period. Especially after the Restoration and in the course of the last one hundred years this has been the case—historical research tending to rectify what had been an original distortion in a "whig" direction. Occasionally the pendulum has swung too far to the opposite extreme, as when students exaggerate the "myth" of *Magna Carta* and come to see in it nothing more than a feudal document tied down to the reign of John. This aberration, however, is more quickly rectified than the original one —for in every Englishman there is hidden something of a whig that seems to tug at the heart-strings. At almost every stage Coke's mistakes would seem to have been corrected by a further achievement of what must be at least one of the historian's aims: the attempt to see the past with the eyes of the past. The whig interpretation is gradually softened by the removal of those anachronisms which were so remarkable in the early 17th-century scholarship.

We have already seen that Cotton, Spelman and Selden by no means shared all the errors of Sir Edward Coke; and, particularly in works that were published at a later date, they adopted views (concerning the antiquity of the House of Commons for example) which were more conformable with the results of later scholarship. The genuine campaign against Coke was carried out in the latter half of the century, when the "parliamentary" cause had been cut loose from the traditions of the country by a revolutionary party. It was carried further after the power of tradition itself had helped to "restore" Charles II to the throne.

Perhaps in the future somebody will do justice to the labours of the redoubtable Prynne—the Prynne who, having suffered for his *Histrio-Mastix* in the reign of Charles I, became disgusted later with the aberrations of the House of Commons itself, and as Keeper of the Records in the Tower took up the cause of "tradition" against the extremists. He showed with great wealth of documentary reference that (for example) the House of Commons had no right to act as a judicial court. He is malignant towards Coke "whose quotations (through too much credulity or supineness) are . . . relyed on by a meer implicit faith", when in fact he "had little time to peruse the Original Records himself, but only the Notes or Transcripts of others". He tells us that Coke had "an excellent faculty above all others I have yet met with in mistaking, mis-reciting and perverting Records, and Law-books too oft-times, which he had no leisure to peruse". Prynne supported the view that the House of Commons went back no further than the reign of Henry III; that the knights and burgesses "after their call to our Parliaments, 49 Henry III, had scarce the name nor power of our House of Commons"; and that the Lower House did not originally possess the right to adjudicate even upon their own privileges or upon improper election returns. Prynne shows that he has a conception of the growth and development of the

Commons when he describes how the Lords under Edward III and other kings used the Commons in order to put a check on the monarchy, while Henry III and Richard II made use of the same body to "suppress" the "Domineering Lords". He attacked the current idea that the nobility were merely the descendants of the Norman Conquerors. He condemned the way in which Coke used a single precedent to create a Law or Custom of Parliament permitting knights and burgesses to go back to their constituencies before pronouncing upon a new proposal that might be put to them by the king.

The Restoration of 1660 allowed the balance to be redressed and once again a change in the political situation had its effect on the development of English historiography. English historical study gained something from this interlude. It had reached the point at which it was ready to progress by the exercise of sympathy and imagination on the other side. A hundred shuttles went backwards and forwards now, piecing together the threads that the Puritan extremists had so wilfully cut in the middle of the century. They joined up English history again after the great gash caused by the Civil War, and recovered continuity for our institutional life, so that healing could take place and normal growth could begin again. The remarkable figure amongst the historical writers in this connexion is Robert Brady. Though he was not original in his view, he put on a firm basis the verdict that the House of Commons went back only to the time of Henry III. He caused an outcry in the House itself because it could now be said that this body had had its birth in an act of rebellion.

Brady writes:

The far greatest part of MAGNA CARTA concerned *Tenents in Military Service* only, and the LIBERTIES which our Ancient Historians tell were so mightily contended for, if seriously considered, were mainly the LIBERTIES of *Holy Church*. . . .

. . . Magna Charta, most of which is only an abatement of the Rigours and a Relaxation of the Feudal Tenures. . . .

That the Barons who caused it to be drawn up never intended it should be of much advantage to ordinary Free-men, or Freeholders, clearly appears by one Article at the very close of it.

The attacks on Sir Edward Coke have a modern flavour:

But *Sir Edward Coke* doth not care to hear of the *Feudal Law* as it was in use at this time, And hath a fine fetch to play off the *Great Charter* and interpret it *by his Modern Law, that was not then known or heard of, And it hath been and ever was, an Art of some Men to interpret and confound New Laws by Old Practise and Usage; and Old Laws by late Usage and Modern Practice;* when perhaps if they would endeavour to find out the History of those Laws, the Grounds and Reasons upon which they were made, there would be found no congruity between them.[1]

---

[1] Cf. "*Sir Edward Coke* cannot own anything of the Feudal, or any Foreign Law here, though it was really made the English Law by Use and Time: He hath a formal way of speaking, the *Law* doth this, and the *Law* doth that . . . abstracting it from any dependency upon, or creation by the Government, as if it had been here, before there was any, and had grown up with the first Trees, Herbs and Grass."

Brady is interested in the method by which the earlier students had come to error:

Many have been deluded into several Popular Errors, by only observing the sound, and common mistaken significance of the Words; by the True Understanding whereof, and of Things done in the Times I write of, they might have obtained a Right Notion of the Government and State of the Kingdom then, which at this day are much changed from what they were".[1]

Finally, Brady shows something of his general posture in a passage in which he describes a certain type of *Turbulent* Men:

. . . such as hold forth to the People, *Ancient Rights* and *Privileges*, which they have found out in *Records* and *Histories*, in *Charters*, and other *Monuments* of *Antiquity*; by these Men the people are *taught* to prescribe against the Government for many Things they *miscal* Fundamental Rights; by these Men 'tis averred, that under the phrase of *Baronagium Angliae*, both Lords and Commons were Comprehended. . . . That *Ordinary Freeholders* often came to *General Councils* of the Kingdom without *Special Election* or *Representation*; That upon a *Change* in the *Succession* to the Crown, there might be *Extraordinary Conventions* of the People to *declare their Universal Consent* . . . and That this was an *Elective* Kingdom which . . . they cunningly insinuate, though they do not plainly *assert* it in terms.

So the battle was joined after the Restoration of

---

[1] Cf. "The meaning of the word Fideles as also of . . . liberi homines . . . is to be known from the Subject Matter where they are used and the words with which they are joyned in Construction."

1660, and on the one hand were the "turbulents", who had already driven the country to revolution and civil war; on the other hand were the "tories", who had already shown themselves on the side of Stuart despotism. At this point the "tories" make an important contribution to historical understanding and sooner or later even those who are whigs must feel compelled to curb some of their initial extravagances. By the end of the century, however, by the year 1700, the "whigs" had won the victory over the Stuart monarchy and had, so to speak, captured the bulk of the nation for their general point of view. They had secured that *their* precedents should in general be regarded as the valid ones, while everything to the contrary should be taken as an unauthorized exercise of power. And still they maintained their initial assumption—they held that the Revolution of 1688 had restored the constitution to its original principles. They did not merely defeat the political designs of the Stuart dynasty—they won a retrospective victory for their interpretation of the middle ages. Indeed they made their conception of *Magna Carta* come true.

Whig History and the English Tradition

The "Tories", when (for example) they return *Magna Carta* to a feudal context, help the cause of historical study by insisting on the differences between the past and the present. The "Whigs", by a similar paradox, lay hold on an eternal sameness in the English system; so that they stress the continuity of our history—their greatest service is not to historiography but to the English tradition. They may select the kind of precedents that they wish to appropriate from the middle ages. (In the 18th century the radicals produce essays in medieval history to support the demand for annual parliaments.) They can decide, then, which aspects of the medieval constitution shall gain retrospective importance through the modern use which is made of them. Like Coke, they may even seek to make a single precedent the ground for a magnificent assertion about the Law and Custom of Parliament. Yet they knit together all the periods of our history—knit modern England with medieval England across whatever rift the Tudor "despotism" might have created. And the history, precisely because it was turned into so flexible a piece of fabric, was prevented from breaking altogether. Indeed it is the virtue of the whigs that they not only bent the history, so to speak, but they made it more bendable for all the future; they made it possible to preserve continuity while taking the 19th-century transition to democracy.

Perhaps the systems of government which France, England and Poland enjoyed in the 18th century were not originally so diverse as we might imagine, but were the differentiated products, the strangely assorted progeny, of what had been a more indeterminate medieval type of constitution. It is very likely that the whigs in modern times gave our medieval system a development which nobody in the middle ages would have been able to predict. Some might even argue that if England had developed into an autocratic monarchy under the Stuarts, she would still have been able to turn back in a similar way and find the seeds of despotism in the same medieval constitution. In the reign of James I some opposition members were taunted in the House of Commons for their industry in the search for ancient precedents. It was suggested then that this was a game which the king could play, and Charles I took the opportunity when he resurrected antiquated laws during his period of personal rule. All we can say now is that the government of England did not in fact develop into a despotism. In any case a tory historiography based on this monarchical supposition cannot exist in England in the 20th century. It is possible to be a tory historian in detail—to be kind to Charles I or Charles II or George III. It is not possible to have a tory structure of English history as a counterpart to that of the whigs.

The whig interpretation could not become the English tradition, however, until a curious inversion had taken place over the heads of both whigs and tories. The ancient view of the whole process of things in time had to disappear, so that history, instead of being an eternal sameness, (even with a natural tendency to decline,) should be able to turn round and face the future, marching in step with Progress and looking for the better things to come. For a long time Englishmen had amended the constitution while purporting only to recover it in its ancient form; had gone even to the point of revolutionary action in order to "restore it to its original principles"; and had made remarkable advances in the direction of liberty, while imagining that they were putting back the clock. It is not clear that we ever entirely rid ourselves of this thrice blessed confusion of thought. The influence of Machiavelli's historical views on 18th-century whiggism tended to prolong the ancient assumptions and to revivify the terminology that had been based upon them.

The idea of progress supervened; but if on the continent it engendered too exuberant an optimism —if men were tempted to tear themselves too wilfully from their historic past so that they flew without ballast after utopias and perfectibilities—still we shall see in our next chapter how this was not the case with Englishmen; how, at the very moment when the whigs appeared to be passing over to doctrinairism, they took, so to speak, a new resolution in favour of the alliance with history. Pegging their tents more safely to the earth, they still kept contact with their traditions; appropriating those aspects of the idea of progress which provided a basis for a new "continuity of history".

It may be noted that the real alternative to whig history in recent times—the real tory alternative to the organization of English history on the basis of the growth of liberty—was the story of British expansion overseas. Attempts were made to give currency to this organization of the story of England, but the whiggism that is in all Englishmen declined to take the imperialistic version to its heart. Now, however, even this structure of the history of England is a tory alternative no more; and only in recent times have we come to see how this epic of British expansion has been swallowed into the original system of the whigs. Perhaps only in the shock of 1940 did we realize to what a degree the British Empire had become an organization for the purpose of liberty. What power is in this English tradition which swallows up monarchy, toryism, imperialism, yet leaves each of them still existing, each part of a wider synthesis. And how cunningly did the whig interpretation assert itself in all the utterances of Englishmen in 1940—throbbing and alive again, and now projected upon an extended map.

PART II: THE POLITICAL TRADITION

∽

I. THE WHIGS IN ACTION

The English Policy of Compromise

Up to the time of Charles II there had been an abundance of "whig history", and the country had taken its plunge through the flaming hoop of civil war and revolution, but the outlook of the historic whigs had not yet emerged. The results of the 17th-century movements were summed up at the close of the century in the emergence of the whig method (which became the English tradition) in the practice of politics—the achievement of that particular attitude or outlook which we generally have in mind when we speak of "whiggism". It is important to us because it reveals—condensed into policies adapted to a given time and place—the discernible implications of the Englishman's alliance with Time and History. It raises the question of the way men can best assert themselves in the historical process, the question of the most effective form of co-operation with Providence. We might say that it expresses the relations of Englishmen with their history, expresses the continuity of past and present, by resolving this into a certain kind of political mechanics; except that the term is too rigid for the description of a method which (among other elements) must involve the subtler form of wisdom that comes from experience, and must depend on what we might call a right feeling for events.

Much has been written of the Englishman's genius for political adjustment, his aptitude for give-and-take, his inclination to compromise, his disposition to co-operate with the trend of events themselves, without too great fretfulness when these are not quite to his liking. Sometimes it has been assumed that the politic nature of the Englishman is innate—a product of climate or character perhaps; as though in the 17th century we had never run to wildness and shocked the world by beheading a king. Sometimes our good fortune has been ascribed to insularity—to the fact that we have escaped that intensity of conflict which has so often afflicted the nations of continental Europe; as though our freedom from fanatical cleavages were in no part due to any exercise of moderation; as though our own 17th century itself had not shown what intensities of passion could be evoked if Englishmen neglected to be politic. We might retort that the French nobility in 1789 did in fact make their concessions just too late to save their order, while in 1832 the English conservatives gave way at least in time to forestall a revolutionary outbreak. Without pretending that any one explanation exhausts the truth of this delicate matter, let us examine one aspect of the case which has at least been insufficiently emphasized, and which is particularly related to the subject of the present study.

To a certain degree at least, the English gift for compromise and for the "politic" management of affairs is itself the product of history. We might expect this to be the case; for indeed no quality is more clearly the result of a ripe experience, of acquired habits and of a seasoned tradition. To an appreciable degree this English characteristic is the traceable product of a discoverable history—a result even that has been self-consciously achieved, the fruit of a deliberate process of reflection upon past mistakes. It descends to us from men who had reason to brood upon the dreadful consequences of wilful and high-handed action in the world of politics. It is, so to speak, the testament of the repentant Englishman who had so early achieved and so soon regretted the horrors of a revolutionary mode of procedure in politics. In a similar way, who could deny that the wisdom of British policy in 19th-century Canada owes something to reflection on experience —to the memory of the mistakes made by George III and his government in their treatment of the American colonies?

There is clear evidence from a foreign observer that the science of a moderate mode of political conduct had become the characteristic of the whigs before 1717. This observer regarded the adoption of the method as deliberate, and he assures us that "the moderation of the whigs is grounded on policy". There is clear evidence that the matter was the subject of deliberate reflection in England at the time of the Exclusion Bill controversy, 1679–1681—a period when some men feared that the country was plunging with careless zeal into a further chapter of civil war. The movement which brought the whole question to the surface was non-party in character, but we may say that in its propaganda it addressed itself to the whigs, attempting to argue with them, so to speak, on their own terms. In its writings, the transition that we have to examine did actually become explicit to a certain degree; there was self-conscious reflection on political method; and the policy of moderation—the application of a kind of brake to keep the fervour of the whigs within bounds—was made the subject of formulated theses.

The Lessons of Civil War

It was the view of Bolingbroke—a view for which there is considerable justification—that the whig party ran to faction in the reign of Charles II, and the tory party in the later years of the reign of Anne. The whigs of Charles II's reign, indeed, were not the whigs that we know—not those of the great tradition—but were violent in their measures, unbridled in their claims, doctrinaire in their attitude to the constitution. The controversy on the subject of the Exclusion Bill brought their truculence and their pretensions to a climax.

It is not surprising that from some quarter or another sober second-thoughts should emerge and should be brought to beat upon the critical situation which was produced. The question naturally arose whether this was the proper moment—and whether this was the appropriate issue—for another civil war. Englishmen who had had reason to deplore the unpredictable consequences of the struggle with Charles I were in a position to brood upon the nature of the political upheaval from which the country had so recently emerged. Those who adhered to the cause of a limited and constitutional monarchy— to the historic rights of Englishmen—could hardly help realizing that the anti-monarchical party itself was in danger of running to tyranny and excess. A party of "trimmers" emerged—not fanatics for despotism or for liberty, but exponents of what might be called a non-doctrinaire system of politics. They were extremely interested in the mechanism of political action, the workings of the historical process, the way consequences proceed out of causes in political history. They were concerned to advertise the dangers of extremism in politics and to study the science of what is practicable. They added point to their teaching by reflections on English history in the period before 1660; also by comments on civil wars in general, and on the events that lead up to them. The result was that in many maxims they gave explicit formulation to the kind of political habits that were to become second nature to the whigs—the kind of practices which made the Revolution of 1688 the most masterly episode in English history. For it should be noted that there is all the difference in the world between the attempted exclusion of James in 1680 and the actual method by which the country disposed of him in 1688.

One of the pamphlets of this period was *The Seasonable Address concerning the Succession, the Fear of Popery*, etc., published in 1681 and attributed (apparently in error) to Halifax. Surveying the course of events from the time of James I, it declares that civil war will be "fatal to the Kingdom in general, to the prince and the subject"; that its issue must be uncertain, to say the least; in fact, "in all probability the King would get the better". It will be time enough to push matters to extremes, says the author, when liberties are actually invaded instead of rushing to arms upon the mere possibility of their invasion. The country must not jeopardize the freedom it has already succeeded in acquiring—must not put everything unnecessarily to hazard—by a rash attempt at further aggrandizement.[1]

Lest we should imagine that the "trimmer" policy is one of mere complacency, implying what we now call "appeasement", or peace at any price, and re-

[1] The kind of brake which the "trimmers" sought to place upon the impetuous forward movement of the whigs is illustrated in such theses as the following:

"'Tis equally destructive of my liberty, whether the King or the House of Commons take away Magna Charta; if there be any choice, the odds is against the latter. . . .

"[The King's] frequent prorogations and dissolutions have been his legal defensive weapons. . . .

"If the people in an island are alarmed that an invasion is designed, and that at only one point, and they become so foolish as for the guard of that to neglect and expose all others, they do but make the easier way for the enemies to land and overcome."

ducible to a preference in favour of the line of least resistance, we must notice the famous *Letter to a Dissenter*. Here Halifax warns the Nonconformists against false compromises with James II and shows why they ought not to make too hasty a treaty with the government, too easy an alliance with the Roman Catholics against the Church of England. Without changing the character of his politics, without displacing the essential principles of his science of statecraft, Halifax illustrates the operation of his methods in what is really a new type of conjuncture. At this point of the argument we are also introduced to an idea or an inclination which became part of the political consciousness of the whigs and which —lurking perhaps in *obiter dicta*—was to become a recognizable element in the political judgments of the typical Englishman: the feeling that, apart from any action we may take in some present conjuncture, the world is changing, and history is moving forward on her own account; and we ourselves must reckon with this process and use it—must conceive of ourselves as co-operating with history, leaning on events somewhat; not resting idly indeed, but lying in wait for opportunity.[1]

[1] Halifax writes: "You act very unskilfully against your visible interest, if you throw away the advantages of which you can hardly fail in the next probable revolution. Things tend naturally to what you would have, if you would let them alone, and not by an unseasonable activity lose the influences of your good star, which promiseth you everything that is prosperous." Halifax then examines the situation to show how Time itself is working to bring about the objects that the Nonconformists have at heart.

Such a non-doctrinaire view of politics will always (from its very character) be deficient in its literary expression, and therefore at a discount amongst academic students of practical affairs. By its empirical nature this science is one which incorporates itself in maxims rather than in elaborate doctrinal structures:

'Tis the highest imprudence to run into real, present, to avoid possible, future evils.

To know when to let things alone is a high pitch of good sense.

In a corrupted age the putting the world in order would breed confusion.

There is reason to think the most celebrated philosophers would have been bunglers at business; but the reason is because they despise it. . . . The government of the world is a great thing; but it is a coarse one, too, compared with the fineness of speculative knowledge.

A rooted disease must be stroked away, rather than kicked away.

Eagerness is apt to overlook consequences, it is loth to be stopped in its career; for when men are in great haste, they see only in a straight line.

Every party, when they find a maxim for their turn, they presently call it a *Fundamental* . . . no feather hath been more blown about in the world than this word Fundamental. . . . For all men would have that principle to be immovable that serves their use at the time.

The Rise of the Whig Tradition

To the enemies of the methods that have just been described there must always be something singularly inglorious in our Glorious Revolution of 1688;

which "owes its peculiar features", as one writer
says, to "the part played by the country gentry,
'trimmers' through sheer necessity". "Rebellion, in
its prospect of possible failure and its unforeseeable
consequences, seemed to such men an unattractive
hazard." For them, however, the headlong course
steered by James II had been "as alarming as the
revolutionary storms through which their boyhood
passed". The result was an attempt to reduce revolution to a mimimum; a resort to the revolutionary
method only in order to prevent something almost
equally terrifying in its promise of upheavals and
incalculable dangers. Yet if Englishmen picked their
way through these times almost as one might balance
and test one's feet across a tight-rope, they did in
fact secure two great objects in the transactions of
1688. What in 1680 could only have been thrown
into the lottery of civil war—and could only have
been achieved after a clash that divided the country
from top to bottom—was now secured by a co-
operative movement of virtually all the politically
effective part of the nation. And what might have
been levered into a trenchant breach of the continuity
of our history, was closed up—was made ready for
the healing processes of time—by stitchings, blood
transfusions and countless little solicitudes. The
result was like the grafting of an appropriate sprig
on to a growing tree. It maintained the continuity
of organic life—a unity more close and rich than
the calculated dove-tailing and the neat geometry of
the carpenter could ever have produced.

The workings of this particular science of politics are acutely described by the French historian, Rapin, in a sketch of the whig and tory parties published in 1717 and apparently written the year before. By this date it would appear that the cautions of the "trimmers" have been adopted by the whigs and have come to be associated with the policy of their party. There emerges into the clear light of day the type of whiggism which became so familiar to historians—the whiggism that chooses only a moderate pace of reform, a cautious progress to whatever end may be desired; the whiggism which, abhorring revolutionary methods, seems now mildly left-wing, now almost indistinguishable from conservatism itself.

It is paradoxical that in his account of the difference between the whig and tory parties, Rapin notes that the tory leaders are the hot-heads—a reproach which Bolingbroke, however, amply confirms when in his writings he looks back to the conduct of the tory leaders—including himself—in the later years of the reign of Anne. (The greatest of all the sinners against the English political tradition were, no doubt, the Jacobites, though Bolingbroke was not referring to these.) The tories, Rapin tells us, cherished vast and dangerous designs, and they betrayed the extravagance of their plans too soon, so that the people knew to be on guard against them. It was true that there were hot-heads also in the ranks of the whigs—the kind of men who had rushed the country to ruin in the days of the Long Parliament, says

Rapin; but now this type of person no longer held
the leadership of the party; he appeared to represent
what we to-day would call the extremist and doctrinaire left-wing. Though they were ready to drive
headlong into republicanism and to impose a presby-
terian system upon the whole country, the zealots
were held on a leash by the whig leaders, who carefully restrained the fanaticism, taking pains to assure
the Church of England that it was in no danger from
them. There was no necessity for the supporters
of the "establishment" to turn tory therefore; and only
occasionally, when the Presbyterians seemed to be becoming too restive, would the whig leaders concede
a point to them in order not to lose their alliance.

The present whig policy (now that the Hanoverian
Succession had been achieved), says Rapin, was not
to hurry forward in the flush of victory, not to make
a drive for further changes, so moving ever to the
left till all was overthrown and a republic established;
it was rather to consolidate the ground already won,
and see that the world became happy and contented
under the new regime; generally trying to make sure
what the times would bear, before unsettling anything else and springing further surprises to disturb
the routine of life. The whigs would take no new
step till they had assured themselves of the positions
they had already gained, and had taken their bearings
afresh in the amended universe.

If the Presbyterians should get seriously out of
hand, therefore, threatening church and state,
threatening a universal overthrow by their immoder-

ate insistence, then the whigs would in the last resort take a conservative stand, and would join the tories in order to preserve the *status quo*. Amongst the tories, even, there were moderate men of similar inclination. If the fiery leaders of this party were to carry their designs beyond the bounds of prudence, some of their followers would tend to go over to the side of the whigs in order to smother this menace to the political stability of the country. It would appear that the ballast in the English system was provided by the moderate, even mediocre, rank and file of both parties—those who repudiated desperation politics or fanatical doctrinairism whether of the right-wing or the left.

Rapin's account was almost prophetic, for it was written before the age of Sir Robert Walpole had really opened. It was to be truer for the whigs of the future than for those of the present or the past. And it was more profoundly relevant than Rapin himself could have realized when he tumbled upon this clue to the interpretation of English politics in the period before 1717. Rapin put his finger upon the essential feature in the recent political education of the class that was to rule England in the 18th century. He gives a firm starting-point for an analysis of what was to become first the "whig", but later the "English" mode of conducting politics.

Under this system a steady, ordered progress is to take the place of desperate conflict leading to revolutionary upheaval. It is assumed that there is much to be thankful for in the British constitution, (for example,) and that this must not be jeopardized in order to forestall purely hypothetical dangers or to hurry unduly the achievement of a remote, precarious or purely speculative good. Abuses are to be reformed—they must be removed at latest before they have provoked the injured or oppressed to a course of revolutionary action. But their removal is to be postponed if it would involve a great tear in the social fabric, or if it would provoke vested interests to desperate measures—even though such measures from the whig point of view were to be regarded as unjustifiable. Beneficent legislation, therefore, might have to be suspended or delayed for a shorter or longer period, if its immediate achievement would divide the country too sharply and embitter political life at the next stage of the story; or if its enactment or its execution would entail too great an exercise of power.

Down to the end of the 18th century the whigs take care not to surrender to the doctrinaire left-wing —not to be carried away by those forces which a prudent politician would rather try to manipulate and control. They might pick out from the radical programme a point that seemed seasonable or right —they were capable of making the cause of Wilkes their own, (though they hated the man,) if the object were a compassable one, not calculated to release the country upon a flood of uncontrollable, unpredictable change. So they performed a curious critical operation upon the programme of the progressive parties, sifting it somewhat and carefully judging what the situation demanded or what the times could bear. And when in 1792 the radicals seemed menacing, so that the whigs had reason to be anxious for the preservation of a system that had been built up in the course of centuries, they would veer over to the right; and, rather than risk the horrors of revolution, they would move almost in a body to the side of the unspeakable Pitt.

The Whig Form of Co-operation with Providence

In general, therefore, the tradition of the English whigs stood for a gradual, ordered progress, the kind that is conducted somewhat as opportunity allows or as necessity dictates. These men knew when it would be best to give way to the pressure of events. They seemed to understand—by tradition and instinct—how to co-operate with history. They did not attempt to force the pace unduly, for they held it as important, among other political objects, to prevent conflict from becoming too bitter or the situation from becoming desperate or events from running out of control. They knew that if they waited awhile, time and a growing reasonableness in men, or perhaps a change of circumstances, would enable them to carry their aim by means less sensational, less heavily charged with danger, less vulnerable to time's revenges. And they knew that there are some evils which, in the words of the "Trimmer", must be "stroked away rather than kicked away"; that, as we can only master nature by becoming somewhat its servant and its ally, so we can achieve things with our history, and our fate, only by a similar humility. The whig stands, however, ready to trap the opportunity when it comes, though he leans upon events somewhat, and seeks to ally himself with the underlying trend of things. At the very worst he is willing to wait even in the darkness for the tide which sooner or later will come to help to carry him home.

If this is not the whig mode of co-operating with Providence—and even supposing it is only the result of a check-mechanism that operated upon the whigs through their clear knowledge of their interests or the firmness of their instinct of self-preservation—it is at any rate the pattern of progress in English history, it is what the English tradition in politics virtually amounted to. Implicit in the system is what we might call a tempered faith in the course of history, provided men do the best they can with due regard to their limitations. Implicit also is the awareness of a ceiling that is not sky-high, a sense of the limited degree to which the ills of the world can be quickly remedied by politics. There is a feeling also for certain imponderable things, certain values difficult to define or locate perhaps, which are ours by the mere fact that we preserve so much of the continuity of our history; so that even when, as in 1688, a cleavage occurs, we actually build bridges in our rear, we seek to join up again, as though it mattered to us to maintain the contact with the past. This whole political outlook further implies a respect for the other man's personality, a recognition of

E

what is due to political opponents, a certain homage to what the other man may think to be a political good. This is the ground and the logic of political compromise and of the English "government by discussion"; and without it democracy can only destroy itself in a conflict of divine right versus diabolical wrong—which in politics can only be regarded as an end of all discussion, a euphemism for a resort to force. The system that we have inherited from the whigs replaces the doctrinaire quest for the highest good by the more difficult search—the enquiry that demands so much more austere self-discipline—the pursuit of the highest practicable good. It implies even a reluctance to force an issue on the mere strength of a momentary acquisition of power—a reluctance to bring things to a decision until something like the general sense of the nation makes itself clear. All these things, so often mute, so often inglorious, weigh heavily on men who have responsibility; but they are mere feathers to the impatient armchair politician. They are aspects of that self-limitation which is necessary for those who seek to co-operate with history.

A French Revolution on the one side, a Hitler on the other side, may of course install a brand-new universe hot from the forge, may impose a colossal "new order" on human beings, if they are determined to do it "whatever the cost". But, granted that in politics things have been achieved sometimes in this way, when men have determined to secure a particular object absolutely regardless of all other consequences, we may say that amongst all political crimes the attempt to fly in the face of history is the one that has suffered the heaviest retribution in the modern world. It is apparent in any case that the whole colossal structure which is raised on human presumption is liable to collapse if the mighty leader makes a single mistake—one mistake in a field of forces so complex that no man can ever be sure that he has reckoned with all the factors. Napoleon was not defeated by men who excelled him in intellect and surpassed him in originality. It is scarcely possible to explain his fall save in terms which imply that as a man of genius he reared himself too proudly and tempted Providence too far. For there is a Providence in the historical process which sometimes (and indeed perhaps often in the long run) is on the side of the mediocrities. And who amongst us would exchange the long line of amiable or prudent statesmen in English history, for all those masterful and awe-inspiring geniuses who have imposed themselves on France and Germany in modern times?

Since the 17th century England has had a happier fate than most of the countries of continental Europe. In particular she has been spared the most violent cataclysms and the bitterness of civil war. There are those who argue that the "whig" pace of progress is too slow—that this whole attitude to politics implies the toleration of abuses (all of which may be described as in a sense intolerable) for too long a period. They think it too much to be asked to wait patiently for a little space—and then still for a little time more perhaps—while the favourable wind lags and hardships continue and the wicked prosper. Most of all, those classes that are without political traditions—and without that brake which the actual responsibility for government imposes—tend naturally to be impatient, over-estimating the amount which can in any case be achieved by political action. For in a sense only those who are the inheritors of tradition can be "whigs"—it takes too long a lifetime for the reckless extremists to learn the errors of their ways. And that is why all must become aware that they are the heirs of a tradition, and must learn something of their inheritance.

Under the whig system, reforms have been overdue on many occasions; yet by the passage of time they have been able to come by a more easy and natural route, and with less accompaniment of counter-evil ; and we have at least been spared that common nemesis of revolutions—the generation of irreconcilable hatreds within the state. And while conflict can be mitigated in this way, the world has a chance to grow in reasonableness. So in fact it has happened that the transition to democracy in England was happier, more assured, less violent than in some other countries of the continent— the whigs possibly serving a better purpose than they knew by standing (as in the time of Rapin) between the radicals and their objective. It is not clear that continental countries, which have had their revolutions, followed by counter-revolutions, have greatly improved on the English rate of progress, in spite of what they paid in havoc and bloodshed precisely for the sake of speed.

Liberal, Conservative and Labour, schooled in the English practice, have mitigated the evils of party cleavage, and prevented the disruption of the state. It has sometimes happened that the tories themselves have carried a reform, which at an earlier period they had bitterly opposed. It is seldom the case that the measures of one party, (when it has its turn in office,) are reversed because a general election produces a change of government. Factors such as this enable the tortoise ultimately to outstrip the hare. One of the most romantic episodes in our history, one of the most gloriously English pieces of story that could be found, one of the most remarkable examples of the success of the "whig" method of conducting affairs, occurs in a working-class movement in the 19th century. It is the impressive achievement of a "Junta" of trade-union leaders, such as Applegarth and Allen, who, after the mid-century, by their wisdom and moderation, and particularly by taking care of the continuities—making history their accomplice—achieved the kind of progress that steals upon the world unawares, and by their wisdom set the trade-union movement on its feet.

In the hands of professional politicians who have no great objects at heart, all this may lead to the politics of pure manipulation. But if there are soulless practitioners of the art—merely seeking adjustment for the sake of adjustment—let us remember that careerists can find cover behind all kinds of political programmes and nature herself, when she cannot move men by reason, will operate sometimes —as in 1688, for example—by means of their personal interests. Though there is always a danger that the pure manipulator, the mere politician, the careerist, may take the soul out of politics, it would be difficult to say that this is the feature of modern English history, or the final verdict which one would give on the whole story. And there has to be some manipulation in a field where well-meaning men differ in their judgments on complicated empirical questions. Finally, though it might be futile to attempt to convince people that there was moderation or virtue in the Congress of Vienna, though all of us might be severe in our criticism of the various kinds of worldly-wisdom displayed in a Castlereagh, a Talleyrand and a Metternich; still, in a peace treaty, diplomatists like these could not send a blind world blundering so quickly into chaos, as would ten righteous men on white horses, rushing with the sword of the Lord to remove wickedness from the face of the earth.

II. THE ENGLISH METHOD AND THE FRENCH REVOLUTIONARY METHOD

Revolution and the Continuity of History

THERE is something in the nature of historical events which twists the course of history in a direction that no man ever intended. And if sometimes men's good intentions are defeated in the process, in a deeper sense we may say that the world gets better in many ways and at sundry times through the action of people who did not realize what they were doing. If we to-day were to mention some of the things that we most prize in the Reformation, and Martin Luther could hear us, he would say that he had never meant his quarrel with the papacy to lead to anything which he considered so wicked and preposterous. It was only to an extraordinarily limited degree that Luther was able to control the consequences of his actions. Nothing is clearer than the fact that the course of history itself, like an overruling Providence, overrides men's plans, takes our purposes out of our hands, and turns these things to ends not realized. When we have made the map of our anticipations and set out all the railway lines for the future, the affair will take an uncharted course as though History herself had stood up and said that she had a right to take a hand in the story. Given such a world in which we can calculate and

are heavily responsible for the immediate consequences of our actions—though the remote consequences are indeed incalculable and may be turned
from good to evil by a hundred intervening factors
—it may be useful to compare the two modes of
co-operating with Providence and of asserting one-
self in the historical process; the English method,
which has been associated with the whig tradition,
or a more trenchant policy—what used to be called
the French method: the revolutionary and the
doctrinaire.

For, just as the French from 1789 trumpeted men's
abstract rights and broke with history and tradition,
while we in the same cause of liberty ran out to
greet the past, taking our stand on the historic rights
of Englishmen—so these two nations, the one
hugging its history close, the other repeating the
old combat in every new present that emerges, have
differed in their behaviour, and in the very texture
of their politics. The French, after the cataclysm
of 1789, did not heal the wounds or tie up the
threads again, did not take hold of themselves and
turn a hatred of violent overthrows into a primary
political principle. On the contrary, with them
Tradition and Reason froze into permanent incom-
patibilities—hardening against one another in order
to produce a standing discontinuity in the very
structure of French politics. The overthrow of 1789
became a matter for glory and emulation—a thing
to be repeated. There emerged therefore a romantic
hypostasization of Revolution as such.

Even now, the historiography of the French Revolution remains in that "heroic age" where men make myths, count their trophies and hold commemorative dinners. And if in our time history ranks somewhat as a general canonical Scripture— to reveal the purpose of God or to confirm men in the faith—within its bounds the French Revolution looms in almost legendary shape; being as it were our Incarnation and Resurrection rolled in one. Here we are to believe that time reveals its purpose —hidden until 1789; as though the Absolute had broken in at last to give us a clue to the meaning of history. Hence, for the modern secular world, *le nouveau Messie, c'est la Révolution*.

This zeal which has run to saga has not been without its disadvantages. In the story of modern liberty the rôle of revolution has been magnified by those purveyors of epics who always tend to over-celebrate a good thing. Save in the case of resistance to a foreign oppressor, the importance of insurrection became something of a superstition, something of a hoax, for the liberals of the 19th century. Revolution, no longer an unavoidable evil or a disagreeable necessity, established itself in its own right, so to speak, as though it were its own end and justification. And, having struck its roots into the earth in this way, it began to sprout and burgeon up above, the hot sap tingling in the twigs till it cracked the bark and then foamed and frolicked into foliage; issuing in conspiracy, assassination, insurrection, bomb-throwings—all the things that are the reverse of the spirit of politics. Like more ancient epics, the story ran to decadence in a species of perverted romanticism. The *reductio ad absurdum* is a form of inverted Quixotry; *vide* the I.R.A.

The Marxists of late have contributed to the current preoccupation with the theme of revolution; though they use the word in a particular sense, and their formula for the historical process does not exclude the idea of gradual change. If in the economy of their system there is a strategic place, a scientifically calculated rôle, and even a marginal necessity, for resort to the drastic revolutionary act—if they argue that some situations allow no other way of escape, and that the historical process at certain crises may need a special lift, a particularly forceful jerk, to get it over one of the hurdles—the whigs can hardly refuse to do justice to such a view of history. But while the whigs believe at least in the possibility of a wisdom, which, combined with good fortune, may prevent the occurrence of such a deadlock— while they argue that the French *noblesse* (for example) might have lacked foresight in 1789, but the English in 1832 found the mere prospect of revolution a sufficient danger-signal—the Marxists on the other hand insist that the revolution, the catastrophic overthrow, is bound to come. They justify their present conduct by this assurance; for whether the revolution is inevitable or not, they are determined to see that it happens and to hurry its coming; and·even before the crisis has ripened they are revolutionaries in advance—setting out to widen rather than to heal the cleavages, whipping up the exasperations, and manufacturing the ultimate hatreds, so long as they can find any fuel at all. They will not risk giving a tactical advantage to the enemy by even allowing the attempt to improve the world by a growth of human understanding. They cannot be happy if by remedying the condition of things a little in our own day, we postpone the end they have set their hearts upon. It will not be their fault at least if their prophecy does not come true. Above all they are Messianic and they show how the human heart, hungering still for the apocalyptic vision, looks to the near future for the fulfilment of all things; yearning to see in these labours and birth-pangs of time the prelude to a great delivery. For they count on a Millennium that will liquidate and wind up for ever the historical process as they themselves have formulated it.

No one can deny the glory and liberty that may be gained by insurrection against an arrogant, unreasoning and intolerable oppressor. If the conservatives and the vested interests do in fact become merely die-hards they may make the whole revolutionary method a cruel and unavoidable necessity. It is also true that 20th-century science, technique and organization give us much greater control of our environment than our forefathers had, enabling us to make vast radical plans of reconstruction, so that we can more completely play Providence for ourselves. History itself may in certain ways become a superstition, and particularly when cataclysm is upon us—when a great war has broken out for example—we may be too enslaved to the past, lacking the elasticity of mind that is necessary to meet the demands of a rapidly changing world. We must not say, however, "It is better that conservatives should be die-hards, in order that we may have the fine flourish of a Revolution". And when we are told to consider the glories of the French Revolution let us not forget that there is a secret treasure of subtle riches which England enjoys as a result of the continuity of her history. Great changes have occurred in this country while deep below the surface the continuity has been maintained as a living thing. And when a cleavage has been made it has not been a matter of mere indifference that—instead of glorying in the cleavage—we have sent the shuttles backwards and forwards in order to tie up the past with the present again.

There was a time when sheer catastrophic interventions and creative acts had a much more considerable part in the explanation of human history than would normally satisfy the student of the present day. The origin of states would be ascribed to a "Legislator". The universe itself sprang into being upon a divine decree. When scientists thought they could achieve their work in a generation— as though it were a mere matter of finding the new lantern-slide to replace the old one—the term "scientific revolution" had a particular potency. Apart from this there is something in the very artifice of the story-maker which has tended to give us too cataclysmic a view of history on occasion. It is more exhilarating to chronicle the victories of one set of men over another than to describe seed-time and harvest or to trace the growth of reasonableness in society. The historian may be hard put to it to show the Providence that works through humdrum intercourse and ordinary discussion, the progress that steals upon the world in uneventful years, the healing that can so often be wrought by time. When revolution breaks out and blood has been shed, here is something that the narrator can seize upon, here is the thunder of a great Event. Hither will come the doctor, the policeman, the finger-print expert, the crime-reporter and the big brass band.

The French Revolution and Modern Liberty

Let it be conceded that the French Revolution threw upon the world a shoal of ideas, experiments, plans and undertakings, the tumult of which—cascading so precipitately—could hardly have descended in a period of humdrum, whiggish progress. In such an epoch of high pressure and febrile fecundity—as in the case of the present war—the course of development is in many ways speeded up, the processes of change become congested somewhat, and we might say that much history is telescoped into a narrow period. Such precocity is not the same as what in peaceful times might be a healthy and balanced growth; and such one-sided developments may for example bring a sudden access of power to men who have lacked the necessarily slower course of moral preparation for its proper exercise. Apart from this, the sheer pressure of the revolutionary situation itself may determine the direction of the prevailing course of change or the character·of the innovations. After 1789 the very state of emergency—as well as the foreign war which resulted from the Revolution— withered the flower of the liberalism and diverted the course to one of "post-democratic tyranny". If the French Revolution produced anything original it was a state organized by the Jacobins for war in a way never dreamed of before in Christian times, a state demanding the full collaboration, the entire absorption, of its citizens; culminating in the Bonapartist Consulate, the dictatorship based on the plebiscite.˙

I do not know who could deny that the French Revolution brought tragedy for the generation upon which it fell—tragedy for France and for Europe not unlike that which resulted from the Nazi Revolution of 1933. Some would argue, however, that the miseries and horrors of the revolutionary epoch were to have their ultimate recompense in the far future— the blood which was shed was mystically to become the fountain of our liberties. To this we might answer that the evils of revolution—the cleavage, the violence, the chaos, the intolerance—are immediate and clear; it is the prospective benefit, the promised recompense, that must always be remote and hypothetical.. If men are able to do so little to control the consequences of their actions in their own day, how shall they presume to make themselves the architects of a dim and highly contingent future?

The fallacy may be illustrated from the case of one of the greatest of the 19th-century preachers of revolution—one who himself had begun by thinking that not only all Italy but the whole of Europe could be overturned almost in a day. Mazzini despised the compromises of the "whigs" and would have no truck with the diplomacy of a Cavour. Yet he came to admit that the programme of insurrections upon which he built his faith implied the sacrifice of a generation. Disdaining immediate objects, reaching far into the future—working for all or nothing—he pointed to the reward that would be enjoyed not by his contemporaries, not by their children perhaps, but at least (let us say) by their grandchildren. Unfortunately, at this very point—in the passage from one generation to another—history seems in a particular way to intervene and to deflect the results of human endeavour; so that we may doubt whether this attempt to overreach Time itself is the proper kind of far-sightedness to have in politics. Apart from new factors that may change the course of the story, there is a process which may give efficacy to the ideas of a Mazzini precisely in so far as these ideas can be made to serve the cause of power; and it is not entirely irrelevant that though Mazzini was no Fascist he did attack the individualism of 1789, and he taught young men to sink themselves—to intoxicate themselves—in the Organic People. One of the things that may happen therefore in the transition to a new generation is the possibility that Mazzini's whole doctrine

—and his glorification of nationality—when mixed with a little earth and entangled in a world of tricks and chances, will form but the raw material for the next Mussolini that may arise. In any case, as we know, the Mussolini does emerge, and the Italians of another age are sacrificed once again for twenty years—still for a reward that is postponed to the end of the story, a reward that is bound to be hypothetical. Sooner or later the Italians will find that these self-immolations, ever repeated for an ever-receding future, have a way of becoming no joke; since so much tragedy can come if a Mazzini or a Mussolini only nearly succeeds, instead of succeeding entirely. Those who play too high a game with Providence are throwing away the present and losing the future too.

After all the noise of the Revolutionary epoch, the progress to democracy did in fact have to be made over again in France, as the slower processes of growth were allowed to operate. After all its revolutions in the 19th century it would be hazardous to assert that in 1943 (or 1939) the political development of that country was greatly ahead of schedule. The extremist revolution of 1848 ran to Bonapartist dictatorship even more quickly than the original outbreak had done; but in 1830, when the example of 1688 was held in mind—when revolution was reduced to a minimum—a successful transition was made to a bourgeois form of government, which was a necessary halting-place; while the foundation of the Third Republic at a time when there was a royalist majority in the Chamber—a provisional arrangement gradually taking root so that the *de facto* was turned by history itself into *de jure*—was the crown of an unspeakably whiggish piece of history. Those who have hoped to reform the Third Republic in recent times have seemed inclined to carry still further the policy then adopted of imitating the British constitution. France seems to have taken a long way round in order ultimately to retreat to this. How much happier she would have been if she could have attained a comparable object by mere unfolding —by a natural course of development—as we ourselves had done. How much richer if she could have held fast to the continuity of her history.

For, in our plans and schemes we take too little account of the imponderable values, the secret strength, that come from this historical continuity. By a too mechanical study of the operations and interactions within the machinery of a state we miss that subtle chemistry which operates in affairs whenever the stuff of human nature is part and parcel of the story. Because many English institutions have century upon century of the past, lying fold upon fold within them—because they preserve somewhat in the present all the previous stages of their being —they possess not merely the kind of romantic colouring which is so dear to the historical novelist, but something like the life of organic creatures; they show therefore greater elasticity in the face of those crises which are beyond prediction than do the paper-constructions of yesterday. Such institutions, in their

sometimes that we should construe so English a system as ours in terms of continental political theory, without considering the dangers that may arise—the conjuring tricks that are sometimes played—when our historic constitution is transposed into formulas that belong to a different world of politics.

The good which seems to come from the French Revolution in after-ages is in any case only the result of human reasonableness playing Providence upon man's past mistakes; for it must be said that, whatever the ills of a generation—whether revolutions or wars or financial disasters—man's reconciling mind in the after-period will operate upon the ruins of the world that remain to it, making virtue of necessity, just as the great Fire of London or the destructive work of German bombers may lead to the creation of a finer city. When the historian imputes great benefits to the Fire of London or the War of 1914 or the French Revolution he is merely using a kind of shorthand; and this does not mean that we were necessarily wrong to fight in 1914 or that the French *Tiers État* were necessarily wrong in 1789: for others may have made the declaration of war or the resort to revolutionary procedure a regrettable necessity. Let us praise, not revolution and war, but man's reconciling mind which acts the good fairy over the worst that human wilfulness may have decreed—which begins to play providence upon the past almost as soon as it has happened, redeeming the mistakes, changing evil into good and turning necessity into opportunity. Let us praise man's reconciling mind—in other words, the wisdom of the whigs, who turned the disasters of our 17th-century Civil War into reflection and experience; and who, precisely because they were lovers of liberty, checked their wantonness and decreed: "This at least shall never happen again".

III. Christian Tradition as a Factor in Politics

Secular Liberalism and its Breach with Tradition

As "whiggism" was taking shape in the way that has been described, a world wearied and torn by theological controversies struck an air-pocket and lurched into the "Age of Reason".

It is customary to take the years 1660–1715 as the crucial stage in what proved to be the most significant transition in a thousand years of history. The movement which was rising in this period was more important than the Renaissance in that it represented a break with much of the ancient as well as much of the medieval outlook. It was so much more important than the Reformation as to render the quarrels between Protestants and Catholics for all the future comparatively irrelevant. Metternich, commenting on the vastness of the resulting achievement—the rapidity of the advance towards "human perfection" —complained that the very wonder which it inspired was responsible for that human "presumption" which he considered to be the root of so many of the evils of his time.

In this movement the methods of the "scientific revolution" of the 17th century were extended to the non-material sciences; and its results were transformed into a new view of the universe, a new attitude to life; all of which was, moreover, greatly publicized and made accessible to the general reading public. A great secularization of life and thought was involved, while technological progress, financial developments and commercial enterprise were beginning clearly to alter the face of the world. It is not surprising that the intellectual changes should have greatly influenced political thinking in the 18th century; producing an outlook which proved to be very different from that of the English whigs—producing in fact the religion of continental liberalism. It would seem that England, as she moved into the Great Secularization, took to the water, still, in her own peculiar way.

Those who were transforming the "scientific revolution" of the 17th century into the "philosophic movement" of 18th-century France, worked under the influence of a great exhilaration and displayed a natural tendency to over-eagerness and haste. Discontinuities are observable not merely between the religious preoccupations of one age and the secular outlook of a later period, but also in a yawning gap between the 17th-century scientists and the 18th-century "philosophers". Descartes, who came to be regarded as the father of the new teaching, complained that his intentions were being twisted and his ideas were being popularly mishandled in his own lifetime. Many of the scientists of the 17th century —Protestants and Catholics—would have been surprised to see the way their work was to be used for the purpose of undermining the Christian religion.

The results of the scientific movement were often popularized and turned into a new world-view not by the scientists themselves but by literary men; some of whom—like their leader Fontenelle—had caught their sceptical outlook not from the sciences at all but by contagion from some ancient philosophy. The course of the new movement could hardly be unaffected by the tone of the "Restoration" in England and the cynical atmosphere of the French Regency after 1715. And discontinuity occurs—there is a break in the line of development (unless it is better to call it a short-circuit) when the new movement fails to capture the universities and the existing authorities in the intellectual realm; with the result that Descartes and others resorted to the vernacular, instead of writing in Latin, in order, as they said, to appeal from the learned world to a wider reading public. Above all, the bourgeoisie—who were always by nature somewhat secular in their preoccupations—were coming into their own in Holland and England, and in the France of Louis XIV. Here is the grand discontinuity—a new class, a class hardly attached to traditions, gained the intellectual leadership. They were ready beforehand to be told that in the gospel according to Descartes a man could only begin to study the universe by divesting himself of all that he had been brought up to believe. So it has been aptly said that the French "philosophic" movement represents the bourgeoisie starting to think.

It is not a straight intellectual development that

occurs, then—the new material being assimilated to the existing body of thought and, after long digestion, producing a modification of the general outlook. Something in the nature of a geological displacement is involved. While men are in the act of taking their bearings the ground is shifting underneath their feet. New verdicts are given not merely because new evidence has been collected but because a new arbiter has dislodged the old one from the seat of judgment itself. The consequence of this hiatus was serious, for it implied that the older tradition was neither gathered up into the new nor clearly demolished—neither absorbed nor liquidated—but merely disconnected. It was left hanging there, so to speak, and therefore Roman Catholicism on the one hand and the new Liberalism on the other began to split the national tradition in France from top to bottom. In consequence of this we have for the future two world-views in conflict; and each tries to find windows into the enemy's system. They can hardly discover the windows, but stand howling at one another from different universes.

Whether it was for the benefit of religion or not, it was a political advantage to England that we were never so deeply sundered by the hardness of this antithesis. We never broke in that definite way with the Christian tradition, and much as it may have declined, we have never quite lost its attendant benefits. Since there was no mammoth hostility (in any wide circle) to harden men's hearts, even those who ceased to be interested in the tradition long

remained tinged with it—haunted in a Words-
worthian way by "intimations" of some sort. Many
things seemed to persist as a kind of hang-over from
the age of faith, even when faith had dwindled, and
it is remarkable how the Christian sentiments can
linger like after-music in the bosoms of those who
would claim to have jettisoned Christian dogma.
Such a religious factor is always a cement to a political body—joining not merely parts of the state
together, but also the history, one century to another.
An American writer, studying English nationalism
in the age of Cromwell, reminds us of the influence
of the Old Testament—the belief that we were God's
Chosen People—which still leaves its mark on the
character of our national tradition. It may have led
us to hypocrisy at times—saddling us with too great
a burden of self-righteousness. But, says this writer,
at least it has prevented English nationalism from
becoming so completely amoral as that of some of
the modern pagan forms of state.

Whatever cleavages occurred at the passage into
the "age of reason", England still maintained the
broad sweep of her continuity. Perhaps it was the
case that, confronted by the new fashions in the intellectual sphere, Protestantism was not so hard a
resisting medium, and so was able to digest more
of the new into the old than was possible with
Roman Catholicism. Perhaps it was important that
in England the churchmen were no mean contro-
versialists and were able to make use of the new
thought in some cases, or to hold their own against

it in others; while in France the church, so distinguished in the 17th century, was inferior in the 18th, too greatly on the defensive, merely hardening into conservatism. Perhaps the effect of the "establishment" in England prevented too great a breach between the church and the spirit of the age; or the existence of Nonconformity helped the progressive party in the state to bridge the gulf between conservative Christianity and liberal thought.

In one way or another the conflict was mitigated and the country was not torn from top to bottom by the warfare, nor was it uprooted from the past. And if some might be convinced that religion itself was moving off the stage, the skirts of a Christian tradition, rich with wonderful pleats and folds, still trailed and rustled across the floor. The whigs did not choose to turn into an anti-ecclesiastical party or to appear as an anti-Christian force. Down to the 20th century the English liberals were affected by the persistence of their alliance with Nonconformity. The churches in their turn, since they were not politically endangered, saw no necessity to lock themselves away in a political die-hard-ism. So the new and the old were allowed to mingle and frontiers were blurred, producing another piece of that English history which, like a weed, grows over the fences, chokes and smothers the boundaries—luxurious and wanton as life itself—to drive the geometers and the heavy logicians to despair. The whigs, and indeed the English in general, were saved from some of the excesses of that secular liberalism which came to prevail on the continent, and which, though never entirely absent here, has not yet been allowed to govern the character of our politics.

The Influence of the Christian Tradition

The divorce of European liberalism from Christianity was accompanied in the first place by the emergence of more optimistic views concerning the reasonableness and righteousness of natural man. Indeed political theory was never the same after it lost the safeguard—or, perhaps we may say, the ballast—afforded to it by the doctrine of the Fall. Under the older tradition the providential institution of the state had provided no cure for the sinfulness of men, but had offered a remedy for the chaos which was due to sin. But whereas this view limits the range of the good that can be achieved by political action, the secular liberals—lacking this effectual brake—have tended to play too high a game in politics; especially as it would seem that all their religion becomes terrestrial, all their faith is virtually compressed into the political field. It is terrifying to think how much even at the present day such people will trust to designs which, before they can be made effective, presume a very general change of heart in their fellow-men; a change of heart that politics, and even the threat of dire calamity, so often fail to produce or can hardly produce quickly enough to meet the occasion. In England, on the other hand, we have tended to be sceptical of the degree to which the ills of the world can be rapidly cured by political action—the degree to which human cupidity may be removed by ingenious arrangements of institutions. Those who have no other political wisdom seem to have a not ill-natured distrust of the fair promises of politicians. Our traditions would hardly have been what they are if politics had been taken as the total sum of our national life and faith.

When he has failed, or when he is in difficulties, the liberal of the continental type too often has only one thing left—his moral indignation. At this point he does indeed pick up the doctrine of sin, but it is important to note that he wears it with a difference; for, as we have seen, he does not commence with it, as the Christian tradition had always done—he drags it from under his sleeve at a later point in the argument. Concerning the sin, of course, he is (as somebody wisely said) "against it": indeed he hates it, not like those who feel implicated themselves, but with the added frenzy of the partisan who has discovered here the totally unexpected obstacle. On this view of life the sinners are indeed fewer in number, but how much wickeder to make up for it! And none is so unforgiving to the transgressors as the person who does not believe in original sin. Here is a system which releases us from self-discipline, authorizing us to treat the political enemy as subhuman, irredeemable. In consequence the good are engaged against the wicked in a more irretrievable warfare, where the makeshift of the ballot-box may itself become intolerable, and nothing is left but the resort to force. Both sides are stiffened in their enmity, possessed by the implacable pagan hatred; and the conflict lacks some of the mitigations, the world lacks some of the fellow-feeling that it had when you began by saying that all were sinners — one touch of nature making the whole world kin.

Such an attitude removes the whole basis for the English system of moderation and compromise; and if our politics have rarely run to these extremes, that is due partly to the traditions of an aristocracy which have expanded into the heritage of the people. When politics bore the character of a struggle between members of a governing class, the result might be bitter and was not always clean, but it was something short of "total war". And though all might have an interest—if they knew it—in the avoidance of a great political upheaval, this governing class were in a better position than most people to see the interest vividly—they needed less imagination to bring it home to themselves. The traditions of the House of Commons, the urbanity that could exist amongst the members of a ruling class, the implicit understanding that in the last resort all conflicts could be resolved into those "quarrels between allies" which are subject to the principle of give-and-take—these did not disappear when English society and government changed their character; for, when the aristocracy was sent to the laundry, the dye ran out into the rest of the washing. Some have laughed at the English for aping the gentry, and some prefer that extremism of the Right or the Left which seeks to proletarianize everybody, reducing politics to naked hatreds. Our latter-day whigs (who at least had the merit of striving for the growth of liberal-mindedness) were more amiable in that they held at the back of their minds the notion that all should be turned into gentlemen. They were wool-gathering when they threw out the idea of "an Eton for everybody" into the bargain, but their dream—the "nationalization" of the best in an aristocratic tradition—has not, in English politics at least, proved quite the joke that it might have appeared to be at first sight. It is thoroughly whig in its conception of a progress that makes capital out of the very continuity of history.

But if the genealogy of the English tradition helps to explain why our political life has been comparatively free from the ultimate pagan hatreds, we must not forget—though it is not easy to measure—the influence which a thousand years of Christianity must have had in a country where it has never been wholly replaced or seriously offset by a flood of militantly anti-Christian tendencies. Such an influence exists, even in the case of people who have forgotten (or who never knew) that they had ever been affected by it; and it might be expected to show itself in odds-and-ends of sentiment, in sundry little biases and in common turns of speech. Perhaps it is the case that Englishmen are not goaded by the thought that they themselves must be drastic since there is no god to do the avenging. Perhaps they are less apt to run to frenzy than those who load the whole of their religion and their faith into their politics. Perhaps they are less tainted by that super-Manichaean heresy which regards live human beings as essentially unreal—mere bodies to ride over on the way to Utopia; which rarifies love of one's neighbour into a veritable passion for everything that is abstract and far-away, and works for a freedom that is anywhere but here and now—a perfect freedom that only posterity shall be allowed to enjoy; as though all our charity must be saved and put on ice for those filmy apparitions, the ghosts of the perpetually unborn. In any case it would be strange if the influence of Nonconformity in modern times had not affected the attitude of the Englishman to the claims of human personality; assisting at least his disposition to concede that "the other man" may after all have good reason for what he does or what he believes. The other man may have his own way of being righteous, though his loyalties are not entirely ours.

One of the incidental advantages of the Christian religion has lain in the fact that it does at least prevent men from making gods out of things of the world, either through fervour or through absence of mind. When men parted first from their Christianity and then from their deism, the deification of the state was bound to be achieved in a comparatively short space of time; for no system can pretend to face all weathers when it has been reduced to naked individualism and the mere assertion of individual rights. Men make gods now, not out of wood and stone, which though a waste of time is a comparatively harmless proceeding, but out of their abstract nouns, which are the most treacherous and explosive things in the world. When human beings lost the unique place which in Christianity they had held amongst all created things, and became no longer the end and purpose of the created universe, but a mere part of nature, the highest of the animals—a more intricate organization of matter than the beasts of the field, but part and parcel of the same system—then, fallen as they were from the dignity of eternal souls, it was easy to think of them as not (from a terrestrial point of view) ends in themselves, but as means to an end; each of them not a whole, but a part of some higher system, some super-person, whether the Volk or the New Order or the deified State. Once that super-personality has been brought into existence, then the Rubicon has been crossed; for nothing—nothing at least in the universe of modern rationalism—can prevent the Leviathan from growing until it has swallowed every right of the individual. The Christian religion itself can be parodied and instead of reconciling our wills to the will of God we are told that we can only find salvation by making the will of the state our own. To this deified state all men must surrender in fact, saying solemnly: "We are but broken lights of thee". How much better for the world if men—so anxious to escape from the wilderness of a naked individualism—had worshipped anything high up in the sky, if only the sun, or an imaginary empty O poised on some other ridge of the firmament. For this, in the 20th century, could hardly have produced the burnings and human

F

sacrifices of that other god, so terrible, and so near at hand.

Not long before the outbreak of the present war a German student set out to show that English writers and orators had often paid tribute to the deified state. It is easy to fall into the terminology of this system, especially in times of stress, when it is natural to urge that love of country makes a total claim on the self-sacrifice of individuals. It is difficult to believe, however, that the English political mentality is sufficiently airtight and insulated to provide a safe receptacle for the German mysticism. What we seem to concede to it in some of our verbal theses is overruled by the nature of the intellectual background against which these things are to be interpreted. The liberals of the continent, on the other hand, first forsook their Christianity, and then set out to cut away the traditions, sentiments, prejudices which they seemed to regard as a mere undergrowth. They did not know that what they were exorcising was their guardian angel and the transition to the pagan state came with remarkable punctuality. The whole system which in the "rights of man" had seemed for a moment to put the individual at the top of the world, cried out in fact to be inverted; it stood asking to be transposed into "the duties of man". And, since the usual cautions were absent, this change—apparently so innocuous and even laudable—turned out to have strings attached to it; for human beings became second to something else in the created universe. Periods of emergency, desperate situations, policies of extremism, tend to hasten this particular transition. Under this kind of pressure the French Revolution—notwithstanding the "individualism" of 1789—became a goddess in spite of herself, floated away from her first principles, and ended by devouring her own children.

Mazzini, when he first founded his Society of Young Italy, expected an almost instantaneous overthrow of the *ancien régime*. He saw his whole dream of revolution shattered in 1833 and fell into a long depression which brought him to the verge of insanity. He emerged from his gloom in 1835, carrying now a new gospel, avowedly religious in character —a gospel that he claimed would transmute souls and bring the Italian nation to its redemption. His problem, he tells us plainly, was to find a cause for which individuals, whipped to the point of rapture, would gladly volunteer for self-immolation. Since they would not put themselves on the altar for the sake of their rights—since they would not sacrifice the greatest of these, the right to life, for the mere sake of securing the inferior ones—Mazzini avowedly sought within the world of politics a formula for which men would forget themselves, he sought to create a spirit like that of the early Christian martyrs. He now attacked the French Revolution as being the end of an old era and not the beginning of a new one. He said that it was merely the last episode in the age of Christianity, the liquidation of the age of individualism. The new revolution, the new world order, would have its capital in Rome and would release mankind from the frost and materialism of an individualistic creed. Mazzini conjured up therefore the conception of a People in which individuals were to sink themselves, and achieve a kind of intoxication. So under desperate stresses, the creed of the secular liberals tends to become subject to a gradual process of inversion. The very weaknesses in that liberalism have assisted the growth of the monstrosities of 20th-century political thought.

Yet no one had more of the after-music of Christianity hanging in his mind than this Mazzini, treading a road that could ultimately be twisted in the direction of Fascism. None of the liberals ever filled the dry lines of a secular system with more of the warmth of Christian sentiment. His regard for personality went far beyond anything that the formal pattern of some of his theses would have justified. Indeed, so much stronger was the sentiment in him than the doctrine, that he never dreamed of "individualism" as being in jeopardy at all—never imagined that, read in a more pagan age, some of his teaching might point the way to the enslavement of human beings.

It is a similar case of Christian hang-over that exists in 20th-century England; and if some writers have slipped into the terminology of modern Germans, yet Englishmen in their hearts have never been worshippers of the deified state. Their hold on their "individualism" is stronger than that of the secular liberals of the continent, because it is rooted in tradition and sentiment. The individualism on the one hand, the love of country on the other hand, are less

likely to be dangerous when growing in this kind
of earth—less likely to devour one another. Even
if our self-rationalization is faulty at times, the error
is of less immediate consequence; for men may sometimes be better than their doctrines precisely as the
prejudices, the sentiments, the traditions prevail.

It was said in the middle ages that God uses inter-
mediate agents to make the material world, mere
animal life and the human body; but he creates every
human soul with His own hands. Human beings,
though fallen from the state of innocence, move as
gods and bear the image of God; they are not part
of the litter of the earth, to be left uncounted like
the sands of the sea. Each is a precious jewel, each
a separate well of life, each we may say a separate
poem; so that, without taking them in the mass,
every single one of them has a value incommensurate
with anything else in the created universe. In the
light of this doctrine, the riches of human personality, the possibilities that lie in human nature and the
fulness of the word humanity itself, were fostered
and treasured by the teaching of the church. Even
if only a shadow of the Christian tradition still hangs
across our path, we can hardly surrender to the
mythology of the deified state.

Finally, if by abridging forms of wisdom not to
be collected in a single lifetime tradition has served
men better than they knew, (endowing them with
another instinct, for example, to make them aware
of the danger-signals,) this was never more important
than in the long currency of the idea of an overruling

Providence. Not man's sovereign action alone governs the pattern which things are taking; but man working on material which itself rebels against him, and working in co-operation with factors that are just not calculable. However well we strive to play our part in the orchestra, we must not imagine that we are quite the composers of the piece. History herself puts limits to our actions and volitions, or at least deflects their consequences; if only by compounding our wills with those of others, or overriding them by forces that are beyond our control; if only by revenging itself on our wilfulness and releasing the fury of the ungovernable storm. We are mistaken if we imagine that some men devised the Industrial Revolution and then decided to execute the plan. When we attack our capitalists as though they had invented the capitalistic system we are merely behaving as children. In a sense human cupidity is behind that system—but, as Engels once showed, it was the cupidity of all men, both workers and employers, and we need not condemn merely those who prevailed in a general competition. And if there was any order, any pattern at the finish, if there was any system to regulate the chaos and even set bounds to the cupidities, this—the "capitalistic system"—came to save us from something worse, and was the work of History herself; it was the work of human reason playing Providence over men's cupidities and past mistakes. This fact does not give the "system" a moment's right to go on existing after its usefulness has ceased; but it should modify any impression we might have of our sovereignty in the face of destiny.

There is a hollow ring in the work of some of the system-makers, who so often assume that we can catch up with History, collect all the factors into our hands—nothing relevant escaping us—and so become monarchs and masters of the course of things. New men—a Napoleon or a Hitler for example—are more prone to this form of presumption than those who have inherited a traditional statesmanship. And, as Mussolini falls, what would he not give for a chance to start over again with the benefit of the knowledge he now possesses? He who thought that, just this time, his cleverness had taken everything into account, how would he behave if he could be back in 1922, with the advantage of this second wisdom which comes too late to those who refuse to learn truth from folklore? The notion of Providence seems to have come into decline, partly because modern science and organization have greatly increased our control, and perhaps legitimately increased our confidence, in certain spheres. The control is far from complete, but while scapegoats can be discovered, whether for the state of society or for any catastrophe that may happen, it is possible to evade the truth that there are in politics some hurdles which the human intellect has not yet found the way to surmount.

But let us be at rest, for whatever the presumptuous may say, Englishmen do not pretend to believe that at the next peace conference, for example, they will re-model the world to their hearts' desire. We can breathe a sigh of relief, for what single head can carry all the varying factors which would give a theoretically ideal settlement of, say, the frontiers of the Central European states? What single head can hold them together, balancing them and collating them, with exquisite judgment at every step of the way, with a reasonable partiality between the contestants, and with none of that arrogance which makes men abuse their power? The leaders of this country know what skill we shall need to secure even some due share in the settlement of some of the controversial questions. It is likely that the share they gain will be larger than it otherwise might have been, by reason of the traditional elasticity of English statesmanship in the face of the historical facts with which it is confronted, and in the face of the providential order. It is good that Providence should have a part in the process, while each man does his best without too great fretfulness; for if any man thinks that he has the solution for the world's problems he speaks too soon and is guilty of over-simplification. If any man says, "I have the only solution that would save the world, therefore all must follow my method, and I will co-operate with no other", he will waste the rest of his life in querulousness, not knowing that his complaints are against Providence itself. And, as he utters the words, a peal of laughter, for all the world like a monkey that chatters and capers and jumps and mocks, will rise in great leaps up the tree that holds the universe; scampering among the branches, and carrying the commotion to the clusters of stars.

Conclusion

At a time when bold enterprises are called for, when vast changes must come if only to rectify the dislocations produced by war, when cataclysm itself (since it is upon us) must be taken as an opportunity for great designs which in peaceful days might have been less practicable, it is not beside the point to reflect on traditions which have survived the great transformations of modern times, and on that continuity of history which we have been careful to maintain even through storms and overthrows.

Members of the audience will now carefully observe that the ragged performer who stands before them carries no hat, has both hands empty, and hides nothing up his sleeve. We cannot say that trenchant decisions in politics are an evil, that revolution is always avoidable, or that insurrection is never right. We may not infer that in a state which has been brought to ruin by military defeat, the presence of a revolutionary party that knows what it wants and goes directly to its end is not a boon to be hoped for, possibly the straightest way out of the existing chaos. We must not forget that the virtues of the whigs have been distributed through all the great parties of this country; that they have liberalized English politics generally, and given a colour to all our progress; standing in protest equally against die-hard-ism on the one hand and mere lust for overthrow on the other.

But, whatever our political objects may be, something in the mode of approach to them does make a difference; and it matters if somewhere at the back of our minds we give a thought to the secret strength which we possess because our roots drive far into the past. There are those who see history as a piece of mathematics and reduce it to geometrical patterns with clean white spaces (where there ought to be rich thick undergrowth) between the lines. In fact it is a living thing, and it resembles poetry rather than geometry; for when you think you have caught it in your net and hemmed it in with your formulas, it continues to breathe with an excess of meaning, as though the best about it had still been left unsaid. Let us praise as a living thing the continuity of our history, and praise the whigs who taught us that we must nurse this blessing—reconciling continuity with change, discovering mediations between past and present, and showing what can be achieved by man's reconciling mind. Perhaps it is not even the whigs that we should praise, but rather something in our traditions which captured the party at the moment when it seemed ready to drift into unmeasurable waters. Perhaps we owe most in fact to the solid body of Englishmen, who throughout the centuries have resisted the wildest aberrations, determined never for the sake of speculative ends to lose the good they already possessed; anxious not to destroy those virtues in their national life which need long periods of time for their development; but waiting to steal for the whole nation what they could appropriate in the traditions of monarchy, aristocracy bourgeoisie and church.

INDEX

DATE DUE

1/20			
GAYLORD			PRINTED IN U.S.A.